Dream Big, Add Moxie
From Flying to Frying to Philanthropy

by Darlene L. Pfeiffer
as told to Debra Bresnan

Copyright © 2022 by Darlene L. Pfeiffer. All rights reserved.
Dream Big, Add Moxie is published by Darlene L. Pfeiffer, who is the sole owner of exclusive rights to the work in all media and forms. No part of this publication may be reproduced, stored in a retrieval system, or transmitted in any form or by any means, electronic, mechanical, photocopying, recording, scanning, or otherwise, except as permitted under Section 107 or 108 of the 1976 United States Copyright Act, without prior written permission of the author. Such requests should be addressed: Permissions, Darlene L. Pfeiffer, PO Box 1185, Port Ewen, NY 12466, or via DarleneLPfeiffer@gmail.com.

ISBN 978-1-387-37987-3

Cover design by Rachel Ake Kuech
Book design by Rick Whelan, DittoDoesDesign.com

Scan this QR code or visit dreambigaddmoxie.com to purchase copies of *Dream Big, Add Moxie* or to send an email message to Darlene.

DEDICATION

*To entrepreneurs and philanthropists
who persevere to achieve their dreams.*

Darlene L. Pfeiffer
2022

Contents

Preface by Darlene L. Pfeiffer vi

PART ONE
THE EARLY YEARS: Planning Fearlessly 1
Chapter 1: Set Goals and Be Relentless 3
Chapter 2: A Positive Attitude Is Your Key 7
Chapter 3: Arise! And Make a List 12
Chapter 4: Speak Your Truth 14
Chapter 5: Show and Sow Appreciation 16

PART TWO
THE TWA YEARS: Flying Fearlessly 19
Chapter 6: A Leader Evolves 21
Chapter 7: Have a Smile for Everyone You Meet 27
Chapter 8: Impress for Success 29
Chapter 9: Stand Your Ground 33
Chapter 10: Who Are You? 35
Chapter 11: Mentor: Jake Gottlieb
    Give Someone Else a Boost 40

PART THREE
THE KFC YEARS: Working Fearlessly 61
Chapter 12: Start Small, Add Moxie and Stay the Course .. 63
Chapter 13: Build Your Own Family 70
    Bevy Hung's Perspective: Part 1 75
Chapter 14: Mentor: Colonel Sanders
    A Recipe for Giving 77
Chapter 15: Keep Moving Forward 86
    Bevy Hung's Perspective: Part 2 90
Chapter 16: Love and Local Service 95
    Nick Pfeiffer's Perspective 99
    Bevy Hung's Perspective: Part 3 101
Chapter 17: The Strength of Family 103
Chapter 18: Securing My Full TWA Pension 111
Chapter 19: Serving KFC Franchisees on a National Level 114
Chapter 20: PepsiCo Takes Ownership of KFC 121

Chapter 21: Capturing the Printing Presses 127
Chapter 22: Building a War Chest for the
    Battle with PepsiCo 131
Chapter 23: A Second Term as President and the
    Final Push to Success 134
Chapter 24: Giving Is Eternal—
    The KFC Scholarship Program 137
    Anreka Gordon: Colonel Sanders
        KFC Scholarship Winner 144
    Paul DeLisio's Perspective 148
Chapter 25: Mentoring Is Giving 151
    Joe Farley's Perspective 152
    Chris Fautz's Perspective 155

PART FOUR
SUNY Ulster: Giving Fearlessly 159
Chapter 26: Focus on the Impact 161
    Bevy Hung's Perspective: Part 4 163
Chapter 27: Darlene L. Pfeiffer Scholarships 164
Chapter 28: Darlene L. Pfeiffer Scholarship
    Recipient Profile: Jill Costello 168
Chapter 29: The Darlene L. Pfeiffer Center for
    Entrepreneurial Studies 171
Chapter 30: The Pfeiffer Technology & Innovation Lab 176
Chapter 31: New Start for Women 179
Chapter 32: New Start for Women: Student Profiles 185
    Rachel Collins 185
    Samantha Wolven 188
    Jill Pacheco 190
Chapter 33: Going Forward 192
Chapter 34: The President's Challenge Scholarship 195

APPENDICES
A Lifetime of Living Fearlessly 198
Credits 204

Preface

Once I decide to do something, I'm all in. This is true of me in business, in love, in investing and in giving. Patience is not my best virtue.

Over my lifetime, I've both created and been dealt many opportunities to grow and overcome new challenges. My childhood wasn't the best, but I didn't let it define the rest of my life. Being a flight attendant helped me understand I could exert control in difficult situations. I wasn't used to being pushed around by anyone, let alone men, and I learned not to let people control me. I didn't brook any nonsense. The years I worked in the air prepared me to go into business, and I knew I had to be strong. Although there were a few other women who contributed a lot to the franchisee group at Kentucky Fried Chicken, I was the only woman really involved in protecting franchisee rights on a national level.

Two people in my life—Mrs. Fleming and Jake Gottlieb—revealed to me the compounding effect of generosity and giving, but I was too young then to fully grasp the message. In my 52 years of working in the Kentucky Fried Chicken franchisee system, Colonel Sanders' philosophy and exacting business standards deeply impressed me. The Colonel showed me and so many others how much influence one person can have—and formed a foundation for my passionate advocacy for scholarship programs, both at the KFC and more recently, at SUNY Ulster.

Over time, I came to understand more fully the enduring impact of giving. My longtime friend and life partner, Paul DeLisio, helped steer me towards good investments to help me build a sizable nest egg. I started small, worked hard, stayed frugal, and set up plans to save and invest my earnings. I put money in and let it grow.

I hope these stories from my life will inspire you to live fearlessly, to persevere and to create meaningful ways to give to others.

The people you give to now will outlive you,
and however you give will influence their lives.

I believe when we give, we live more fully.

When we give, we live completely.

When we give, we live more joyously.

And when we give, we live eternally.

Darlene L. Pfeiffer
December 2021

Portrait by Michael Gold

CLOCKWISE FROM ABOVE
Darlene 6 years old; 8 years old – when Darlene set goal to be a flight attendant; one of the houses Grandmother Large built at turn of the 20th century: high school graduation 1955; and prom date 1955.

FACING PAGE
*Top – (L-R) Robert Large, mother, Darlene. In front of their house Easter 1951.
Bottom – Andre Correlli Modeling School mid-1950s.*

PART ONE

The Early Years
Planning Fearlessly

• 1 •

Clockwise from above: Darlene 2 years old; Otto Large (father) at airfield at Port Columbus before he flew to California to visit his ailing mother. It was when Darlene set her goal to be a flight attendant; junior high school graduation 1952.

CHAPTER 1

Set Goals and Be Relentless

*No matter what you want to accomplish in life,
you have to set goals, believe in yourself and persevere.
Do not give up, no matter what happens.*

I was born on October 6, 1937, and was raised in Columbus, Ohio, where I lived with my mother, Louise; my father, Otto; and my older brother, Robert.

I like to tell people I was "born in a hurry." My mother was given twilight sleep, the latest and greatest form of natural childbirth. Using twilight sleep—a mixture of morphine and scopolamine—allowed women to deliver babies without memory of pain, a new thing in those days. My mother was lying in bed at the hospital, not in the delivery room. Her sister, my Aunt Eloise, heard a gurgling noise, lifted the sheet covering my mother and said to the nurse, "Shouldn't she be in the delivery room?" Five minutes later, I popped out, fast.

I've always been in a hurry. My second husband, Wally, would say, "Where are you going?" and I would say, "I don't know. Just get out of my way." Nowadays, my life partner, Paul, always tells me to slow down, but I'm just wired to be in a hurry. I got it from my grandmothers: nobody else in my family was that way.

I think we inherit a lot of who we are, and I am a great believer in genetics. My Grandmother Bailey, my mother's mother, was the daughter of a Methodist minister in Texas, and she made horse blankets around the time of World War I. She was a giving, spiritual being. She held me in her lap as she sat in her rocking chair and talked with me about Jesus and Bible stories, which offered me a little spiritual training. She died when I was eight.

My other grandmother, my father's mother, was an entrepreneur. Grandmother Large—Largé if you want to get fancy—was a contractor who built houses in Columbus at the turn of the century. She raised seven kids, basically alone. Neither of my grandmothers' husbands contributed much to the family.

Columbus, the capital of Ohio, was a pretty city when I was growing up. It had huge state capital office buildings, a large insurance tower, and good bus service downtown, which was important because our family didn't have a car. About 300,000 people lived there then, so it was the third-largest city in Ohio, behind Cleveland and Cincinnati.

When I was eight years old, I set my sights on becoming an airline flight attendant. It was going to be my ticket to see the world.

I got the idea when my father and mother took me to the airport with them. My father was flying to Burbank, California, to visit his sick mother. This was 1945, right after the war, and in those days, you could stand practically on the field. The plane was a DC-3, and there was a beautiful young lady greeting passengers on the ground. I asked my mother what she does.

"She's a stewardess," my mother said, "and she flies all over the world, serving passengers."

"That's what I want to do."

From then on, everything I did was focused on becoming a flight attendant. People often get too consumed by their daily routine, and don't make lists or set a path to accomplish important goals. Since the age of eight, I've always had a laser beam fixed on what I want to accomplish.

I went to the library to read about the requirements to become a flight attendant, and learned it was very difficult to be accepted.

While I was still in high school, I took up modeling in my spare time to learn to walk and dress right and to add substance to my resume. I enrolled in the Andre Corelli Modeling School in Columbus and attended classes on Saturdays for six months.

When I told Andre I was grooming myself to become a flight attendant, he said, "Don't ever do that. Flight attendants are just waitresses in the sky. It's a horrible job. You could be a great model, an actress, anything but that!"

"Well, that's what I want to do, and I'm going to do it," I said.

Andre was extremely strict with us and observed everything we did with a critical eye. One day he thought my bra strap looked dirty.

"That's not attractive at all, Darlene," he told me. "It's not clean. Don't ever, ever, EVER do that, Darlene."

Andre said things like that to us all the time. I learned how to walk, how to dress, what would look attractive on me, what neckline was most flattering, how a dress should fit me, and how to act like a lady. I bought a lovely little black dress—an evening dress with a pretty neckline—and after he complimented me, I wore it constantly.

Since it was an arduous process to become a flight attendant, I had to prepare myself fully, including developing a Plan B. After I graduated high school as class valedictorian, I enrolled in college because the airlines preferred flight attendants to have some college. If I couldn't get into the airlines, my fallback plan was to become a teacher.

In the summer of 1957—12 years after I had set my goal—the airlines sent a representative to Columbus. I applied and was interviewed, along with a few others from my class at West High School. No one else from Columbus was selected except me. Once I passed my first interview, I flew to Kansas City for a second interview. The airlines only accepted about one out every 500 women who applied nationally, and my persistence paid off: I was accepted to enter the flight attendant training program.

After I completed my training, I moved to New York City and began flying in January of 1958 when I was 20 years old. I worked 80 hours a month, about 20 hours each week, on domestic flights all around the United States.

DARLENE L. PFEIFFER

I loved being a flight attendant. I loved traveling, the airline industry was new, the women were beautiful, and you could attract any man you wanted, really. I loved the freedom and glamor of the lifestyle, the faraway, sentimental journeys, all of it. It was like the first line—"See the pyramids along the Nile"—from "You Belong to Me," which is one of my favorite songs.

From the time I was a young girl, I had known I wanted to be a flight attendant and I had let nothing stand in my way to achieve that goal. A lot of people will tell you to "keep your eye on the prize," and I'm here to say that if you do, you'll get what you want. It may not be easy, and it may take years, but if you don't waver and you keep at it, you'll get there.

Fly high with your dreams!

CHAPTER 2

A Positive Attitude is Your Key

*Fighting obstacles can make you stronger
and have a positive impact on your development.*

My father was an alcoholic. There was a lot of fighting and discord in my home when I was a child.

My mother kept the stove turned on and a pot of water on the burner, so if my father threatened her, she could throw boiling water on him. I'd run to turn off the burners because I didn't want him to get scalded. That's the kind of childhood I had—domestic violence and alcoholism—but I overcame it.

When I was seven or eight years old, I remember standing out in my yard—a small lot that seemed huge to me. My daddy raised chickens and as I stood out in the chicken yard, I looked up at the sky and said, "God, what do you want me to do? Why am I here?" I still pray today and ask Him to let me know how to serve. He has guided me all the way.

We moved to a different house when I was 10, and it was only a block from the Evangelical United Brethren Church, which morphed into the Methodist Church. I walked to church and I sang in the choir. My parents never went to church, but on Sundays, I got dressed and ran around my neighborhood, asking if I could go to church with other families. That was my first religious education, and it was varied: I went to the Baptist, Methodist, Lutheran and Catholic churches because my neighbors were of diverse religions. It gave me a strong religious foundation, and that's when I started believing in serving God.

My mother's twin sister, Eloise, lived next door, and my cousin Sue and I had a lot in common because her father was an alcoholic too. We liked nature, going to the creek, playing in the yard, and making something out of nothing. We had no money, few toys—I got a new doll once every year or two—but Sue and I saved all year long—sweeping porches, shoveling snow and things like that—until we had enough to buy a $10 season pass to the swimming pool in summer. Sue was a couple years older than me and we were close all our lives. We talked on the phone every day until she died in 2014.

My father died when I was 13, and my mother was angry because he didn't leave her any insurance money. He didn't believe in insurance, and he died young. She said terrible things about him, constantly.

"Please, don't talk about my dad this way. I loved him."

"No, you've got to hear it because he was no good," she replied. "He left us with nothing and now I have to work."

There have been a lot of studies about children of alcoholics, and the older child is often aloof, ignores the situation and just gets away from it. My brother, who was five and a half years older than me, was always gone, so it was just the two of us, my mother and me.

Mom was a homemaker until Daddy died, and then became a keypunch operator for the State of Ohio. She didn't make much money, so our life was a struggle. I became an adult really fast. I started doing all the cleaning, grocery shopping, cooking and our household budgeting, including preparing federal income tax forms for my mother. I was sad to lose my father, but everything after his death was great training for me. I learned to cook well and shop on a budget. I developed a great proclivity for always finding the good in everything. Now, when somebody dies of a heart attack, I say, "Well, they didn't suffer. It could have been cancer."

I didn't suffer.

My mother was a selfish person, and never seemed to like me. Her twin sister, my Aunt Eloise, told me, "You know, she never wanted you. You talk to her. Ask her."

When I asked her, my mother replied, "No, I didn't want you. Why would I want another child with my alcoholic husband?"

For the first year of my life, she had left me upstairs. Later she told me, "Well, it was warm up there. I did feed you and change your diapers."

A few years ago, I went to see a psychic in Woodstock who asked me, "Did your mother not care for you? Did she treat you strangely?"

She did. I did everything for her, bought a beautiful house for her, took care of her, but I could never do enough.

The psychic said, "Well, you were together in a previous life, during the days of the Romans, and you were her husband then."

I learned that when the Romans wanted to defeat a certain people, they didn't kill them or wipe them out by pillage and plunder. They joined the colony. The Roman soldiers married the women and raised families to make them become a true Roman colony.

The psychic said, "That's what you did when you were her husband. She resents you, and she doesn't know why. Your mother's psyche resents you because that's what you represent to her."

My mother was a strange, funny woman. On my birthday, she would say, "You should celebrate me. I'm the one who gave birth to you. Why should I celebrate you?"

I believe you can overcome an early start like mine. I've had a wonderful life. You can't go through your entire life saying, "Dad was an alcoholic" or "Mother didn't give me much love or attention," and blaming your problems on others.

My childhood made me stronger and had a positive impact on my development.

Maybe it's in my genes to have a positive attitude.

My uncle, Foy Large, became a celebrated, world-famous acrobat and vaudeville star, despite losing his leg when he was 10 years old. He was my father's brother and lived with my Grandmother Large and his six brothers and sisters. As an amputee, Foy had a hard time making enough money to support himself, but he made the best of it, like buying one pair of shoes to share with a fellow newspaper sales boy, Frank Morgner, who had lost the opposite leg. At first, Foy was just being practical, but then he trained Frank to do acrobatics. The two of them entertained other kids by walking on their hands and doing flips, and then they joined the circus together.

Foy Large and Frank Morgner became a well-known vaudeville act and performed on stages all over the world. Variety dubbed them "one of the real novelties of the season... [they introduced] themselves in humorous fashion and then proceed[ed] to astound the audience with their equilibrium ... stopped the show deservedly." In March of 1933, a critic for Zeitun-Berlin newspaper called their act "One of the most unusual acts ever present at the 'Scala' ...perfect synchronized movement gave effect of Siamese twins ...sensational gymnastic work drew for them the greatest applause of the evening." They made it into *Ripley's Believe It Or Not* that year, too: "One suit of clothes does for both Frank Morgner and Foy Large."

I was fascinated by my Uncle Foy when I was a child, and as I grew older and encountered some of my own life challenges, I drew strength from his determination. Foy didn't let hardship stand in his way; instead, he used it to his advantage. This set a great example for me as I faced adversity over the years.

One of my favorite stories is about a mother who took her two boys to see a psychiatrist. She was worried about them because one was an extreme optimist who was always happy, and the other was an extreme pessimist who was always glum. The psychiatrist first put the little pessimist in a room with a one-way glass. The room was full of horse manure. The boy began screaming and crying and became hysterical. He begged to be let out of the room.

After he exited the room, the psychiatrist put the optimist in the room and closed the door. The little optimist became immediately gleeful, began throwing horse manure around, and had a great time digging around in the muck. When he came out of the room, the psychiatrist asked him, "Why were you so happy?"

"With all that horse manure, I knew there had to be a pony in there somewhere," the boy replied.

I am an optimist like that boy. Fighting obstacles made me stronger. When you believe in yourself and take responsibility for your own life, you can find ways to transform challenges into favorable outcomes—if you have a positive attitude.

Remember to look for the pony in every situation.

Foy Large and Frank Morgner.

CHAPTER 3

Arise! And Make a List

No matter how small your goals for each day may seem, set at least one goal to accomplish every day. Then allocate the time for it. When you block out the time necessary to complete all the steps to meet your goal, it becomes realistic and achievable.

When I was growing up, my cousin Sue and I played together all the time. Since Sue was a bit older than me, she was the leader and made sure I knew it.

Sue always had a dog. Her first dog, Taffy, was a scroungy-looking mutt, but then she got a collie she named Lassie, after the popular *Lassie Come Home* movies.

I wanted a dog so badly! Sue said she would sell Taffy to me. Our local bank had a program for kids who wanted to start a savings account, so I put a dime into my account every week. I was determined to have a dog of my own. I had saved about a dollar when Mrs. Jones, who lived across the street and raised cocker spaniels, presented a much better deal to me.

"If you promise to take care of one of my dogs when I go away," she said, "I'll give you one of my puppies." I eagerly accepted her offer.

When the puppies were four weeks old, I got down on my hands and knees and one of them came right over to me. That's how I fulfilled my life dream and got my first dog, a red cocker spaniel I named Chips.

Chips was a beautiful dog and he lived with me for eight years. He was my constant companion, and I spent all my time training him. He learned to ride in the basket of my bicycle. I had my own dog to take down to the creek with me. Chips was my joy.

One of the biggest lessons I've learned—and it all started with taking care of Chips—is to block out time for what I need to do. It's one of the largest contributing factors to success or failure. I started making daily lists, like this one:

Arise: 7:00 a.m.
Feed Chips: 7:30-8:00 a.m.
Walk Chips: 8:00-8:30 a.m.

My whole list was devoted to taking care of Chips!

Ever since then, I've made lists every day. Before I go to bed each night, or first thing in the morning, I set goals for my day. These goals are above and beyond my daily living routine. Taking care of Chips taught me a great deal about responsibility, the joys of caring for others, and how to plan my day. As I matured, daily lists helped me make sure I accomplished tasks and moved forward to reach my goals. When I ran my businesses and assumed leadership roles in the National Association of Kentucky Fried Chicken Franchisees, making a daily list insured that I kept everything, and everyone, on track. I had to be organized and block out the time to do the tasks to accomplish what was most important to me.

I strive to make my daily tasks reasonable and achievable. A list with 50 items is overwhelming and unrealistic. I prioritize my time, so I have enough for each daily task I want to advance. It's amazing how much you can achieve by focusing on only the most important things every day, whether it's taking care of a beloved pet, negotiating a better deal from a business supplier or calling three executives to secure their support for a fundraising campaign.

My lists help me achieve larger goals. If I want to launch a new project by the year's end, I create monthly and weekly benchmarks, so I know the daily steps necessary to be successful.

I like to use the word 'arise' to start my day. It is one small way to reinforce my belief in the importance of looking up and keeping a focus on positive action.

Arise!

CHAPTER 4

Speak Your Truth

Whether the action you take is a not-so-subtle poke in the ribs or a public statement, speak up when you know you are in the right. Your truth telling may help pave a smoother road for those who come after you

When I was 15, I got my first job as a checkout girl at Kroger's. Danny and Dave Krebs were my schoolmates, and their father was the store manager. I rushed there from school, put on my uniform in the bathroom and went to work at the front counter. After a couple of days, Mr. Krebs said, "It's so nice to have you here with us. You're like a part of the family."

Then he hugged me.

One can tell when a hug is inappropriate. He didn't grope me, but it was a little too tight.

The next day, I carried a broom with me, and when he hugged me, I gave it to him in the ribs. He asked me why I carried a broom.

"Mr. Krebs, I must always have a clean workstation," I told him, "so I sweep it before I start working."

I don't know how I knew to do that. It stopped him, but I only lasted there two weeks.

For my next job, I went to work for Beneficial Finance, which was on Main Street in Columbus. I was 16. Ray was my boss, and one other woman worked there. She was full-time and I worked part-time. Customers came into the office to make payments. A card was put in each file to record the payment, and Ray hired me to file the cards.

One day, a supervisor, Mr. Suplee, came into the office. He was a crude person. He pointed at me and said, "Ray, you stupid son-of-a-bitch, what's SHE doing here? You don't need her. Get rid of her."

What could Ray do? His boss had told him to fire me and so, even though he thought I was doing a good job, Ray did

DREAM BIG, ADD MOXIE

what he was told.

Afterwards, I got a survey in the mail asking me about how I enjoyed working at Beneficial Finance. I wrote a nice reply back and included details about Mr. Suplee. I wrote, "He is very unprofessional. He uses profanity constantly and demeans the people who work for the company."

Mr. Suplee got demoted for this, and Ray hired me back. I worked at Beneficial Finance for a couple of years, part-time, and once during that time, Ray took me to a company dinner.

Mr. Suplee was there and as soon as he saw me, he pointed at me and started screaming, "YOU! You got me demoted! I almost got fired because of you!"

"Well, did you stop using profanity?"

I was just a young girl, but I already had a lot of guts. What I wrote on the survey was the truth. I had no experience, but I knew it wasn't right to speak to employees like that. That was one of the first times I felt confident about speaking up for what's right.

Today, in the era of #MeToo, and with increased legal protections against sexual and other types of workplace harassment, women and girls have more rights than they did in the 1950s.

I stood up to those two men who held power over me when I was just a teenager and learned an important lesson: If you are confident and truthful, it is right to speak up.

At the time Darlene got Mr. Suplee demoted in her first job at Beneficial Finance.

CHAPTER 5

Show and Sow Appreciation

A simple 'thank you' offered and received can have a ripple effect. Showing appreciation and using gratitude to focus on the needs of others adds purpose to life.

When I graduated high school as valedictorian in 1955, I was offered two major scholarships. One would have paid for one year at Ohio State University; the other was from Buckeye Girls State, an organization run by the Women of the American Legion Auxiliary of Ohio, and it covered a year of attendance at Capital University.

I learned about the latter scholarship when I attended a weeklong program hosted by the American Legion at Capital University. The highly competitive educational program attracted 500 junior and senior high school girls from across Ohio who wanted to learn about the duties and responsibilities of good citizenship and how state government works. One person out of all the girls who attended the Buckeye Girls State program was chosen to receive a $500 scholarship. I won their coveted Philip Bruck Fleming Scholarship and decided to attend Capital University, which was located in a suburb of Columbus.

Philip Bruck Fleming had been killed in France while fighting in the trenches during World War I and his mother established the scholarship to honor her son. During my first year of college, I visited Mrs. Fleming to convey my thanks. I took two bus lines to go downtown and then transfer to a bus to another part of town.

Mrs. Fleming was an elderly woman, and when I walked into her living room, I noticed right away a photograph of a young man dressed in a World War I uniform looking down on me from her mantel.

"That's my son, Philip," she said when she saw me looking

up at the photo. "He was killed in the war. I have given this annual scholarship for many years in memory of him."

Seeing Philip looking so young and handsome in his uniform made a lasting impression. I stayed for an hour to visit with Mrs. Fleming and she was so thrilled that I had come to thank her that she gave me another $500 for my second year of school. My good manners impressed her—no one had ever thanked her for her scholarship award before then.

My education at Capital University, one of the oldest and largest Lutheran-affiliated schools in America, provided me with a strong religious foundation and became a major turning point in my spiritual education. At Capital University, we were required to take religious training once each semester and to attend chapel three times each week.

My faith has been a guiding force throughout my life, and my religious education at Capital University set me on a path of spiritual growth. Prior to receiving religious instruction at college, I had attended different churches on my own and with my neighbors, and sung in a church choir, but taking college-level courses strengthened my religious foundation. Mrs. Fleming's gift nurtured my growing conviction that we must be of service to others and dedicate our lives to giving.

Receiving her two $500 scholarships had an impact on me that was much deeper than simple financial support.

Mrs. Fleming honored her son and remembered him with love by giving an annual scholarship in his name, and her gift left an impression on me. Her support inspired me to establish scholarship programs through the Kentucky Fried Chicken Colonel Sanders Scholarship Program and at my local community college, SUNY Ulster. Like me, the students I've supported wished to attend college, but needed financial assistance. Each of them had personal and unique goals, and higher education helped provide them with a stronger foundation to achieve success.

CLOCKWISE FROM ABOVE
Darlene, 1957 (20 years old) when first accepted as TWA Flight Attendant; first fur stole – a gift from Jake mid 1960s; and Darlene standing atop the hoods of two Cadillacs from Jake, mid-60s.

FACING PAGE
Top – TWA Flight Center building at John F. Kennedy International Airport; bottom – Ed Sullivan, Darlene, her mother 1964.

PART TWO

The TWA Years
Flying Fearlessly

Top – TWA flight attendant school graduating class – December 1957.
Darlene, front row, 3rd from left.
Bottom – Trans World Airlines Lockheed L-1649 Starliner.

CHAPTER 6

A Leader Evolves

People like to use the phrase "born leader," but leadership requires faith, confidence and a belief in oneself, plus tenacity. You must put these qualities to work—and keep others' best interests at heart— if you want to take the reins and inspire others to follow you. Anyone can become a leader once they commit to taking tiny, brave steps, over and over again.

I completed two years of college before I was accepted into the 30-day training program to become a flight attendant in December of 1957. I was just two months past my 20th birthday. There were 20 of us in the class held at TWA headquarters in Kansas City. The school separated us into groups of four and each group rented an apartment. None of us had lived away from home before and my three roommates were from California, Massachusetts and Pennsylvania.

We would be paid $180 per month, but we had no advance. None of us had any money. We needed our limited funds for rent and bus transportation to class—and since we were responsible for our own meals, that didn't leave a lot of money for food. We needed a plan to survive.

"Do any of you know how to cook?" I asked.

None of them did.

"Well, do you at least know how to make Jell-O?"

They didn't.

That's when I took charge. They didn't even know how to boil water, for God's sake. They didn't know the first thing about how to cook, much less how to live on a budget or shop for groceries. From the time I was 13, I made meals for my mother, my brother and me, but this was on a larger scale.

"I know how to cook, so this is how we're going to do it, girls!" I said. "I'll make lunch and dinner for us every day."

It wasn't like today, when people can get takeout meals or prepared foods, and besides, we couldn't have afforded to eat like that anyway.

Since we were busy in classes from 8:00 a.m. until 6:00

p.m. every weekday, I had to plan ahead so we could eat when we got home from a long day at school. Anything that required more preparation or a longer cooking time, I made on Saturday or Sunday. I made complete meals each weekend so food could just be warmed up and served throughout the week.

We ate a lot of oatmeal in those days and I cooked inexpensively. I knew how to stretch a chicken for two or even three meals by saving the bones to make soup stock and by using leftover roast chicken for sandwiches for lunch the next day. I made meatloaf, stews, soups and spaghetti. If I made a pot of chili, I'd bake cornbread to stretch it even further.

Our meals were simple, yet nutritious. No one said they didn't like it—"This is what we have, girls," I'd tell them—there wasn't a choice and it all worked out great. I just did it and I don't recall teaching anyone else how to cook. Pat McSweeney, my roommate from Massachusetts, told her mother, "We even eat leftovers instead of throwing them out!" Her mother never served them.

I was thrilled if a date wanted to take me to dinner, and since we served meals to passengers on our first-class flights, I would help myself to leftover passenger meals if they hadn't been touched.

We all passed the training program, got our wings and became lifelong friends. Once our training was completed, Pat and I were both domiciled in New York and decided to rent a place together. Neither of us had ever been to New York City. We learned that Queens was less expensive than living in Manhattan and was more convenient for flying out of LaGuardia and Idlewild Airport (which was renamed JFK after President Kennedy was killed).

The airlines gave us only five days to find a place to live before we started flying, and we didn't have a clue about how to find or rent an apartment. On the flight from Kansas City to New York City, I asked our flight attendant how to find a place to live. She had just moved to Queens two months prior and she gave us the name of her realtor. The sisterhood of flight attendants was valuable because we were all operating by the seat of our skirts. I trusted her advice.

The realtor connected us to Guillermo ("Willie") and Osea Gomez, a lovely couple who had emigrated from Cuba a few years before. They owned a three-story apartment building that wasn't finished yet. It was located near the bus line. That's all we knew when we first met them.

Willie and Osea had never had a tenant before, and we had never had a landlord, so we were all a little afraid of each other and nervous at our first meeting. Osea wore a brightly colored bandana tied around her head and didn't speak English very well. But when she said, "You take care of me, and I'll take care of you," that was that.

Willie and Osea got us a couple of single beds and a sofa, and Pat and I moved into a third-floor apartment while work was being done on the first two floors. When I wasn't flying, I oversaw the construction and went to wherever the contractor was working to pepper him with questions. Sometimes I sat on the floor to eat while I watched his every move. He was a hardened New York City man in his 50s, pounding nails in walls to make a living, and I'm surprised he didn't tell me to get lost.

"Why are you doing that?" I would ask with more authority than I felt. "What's the next step? How long will it be until the paint dries?"

I didn't know a damn thing, but I let on I did. He probably thought, "Who is this, bugging me while I'm working?" But I remembered what Osea had said and put myself in charge of taking care of the building. The contractor knew the Gomezes were immigrants and I was just a girl from Columbus, Ohio, but I wasn't going to let anyone pull the wool over Osea's eyes.

I had said I would take care of her, and that was that.

Whenever I came home from flying, I'd stop in to say hello to Osea. One day, she had a big pot of black beans bubbling on the stove.

"Ooh, that's interesting. What are you cooking?" I had never seen black beans.

"How about having some?" she asked.

"OK, they smell delicious," I said and took the bowl she gave me upstairs. I loved it. I didn't really learn to cook from her—she never used recipes and just threw ingredients together—but her cooking was wonderful.

Osea worked as a machine embroiderer for Bergdorf Goodman in the fur department. Her mother cared for her little girl, who was eight months old when we moved into the building. Osea's daughter later became an American Airlines flight attendant—maybe she followed in my footsteps because when she was a toddler, I used to give her my hats to wear. Wealthy women hired Osea to monogram their names in the linings of their fur coats, and she also created elegant embroidery for pillowcases and sheets. Willie was in the importing business and was a very intelligent, handsome man.

I became very close with Osea and Willie and we all had a lot of fun together. They invited Pat and me and all their friends, which included a couple of Cuban doctors, to their parties every Saturday night, and there was always lots of laughter, music, dancing and food. I became part of their big happy family and learned to dance to Cuban music. Osea taught me how to feel the beat for the rumba and lots of other dances, and I still love Cuban music. I've been told I dance as well as a native Cuban.

In October of 1958, Pat and I—like 300,000 other American tourists that year—flew to Cuba for a vacation. On the day we landed in Havana, the airport had just been bombed. Willie had told me lots of stories about Fidel Castro, who had not come to power yet, and how everybody was in favor of him and his revolutionary forces. Castro and his guerrilla fighters were operating from encampments hidden deep in the jungles surrounding the Sierra Maestra, and like most Cubans, Castro's rebels were appalled at the human rights abuses of the then-President Batista, who was a horrible dictator.

We had flown from New York to Miami, where we had a one-night layover, then continued on to Havana. The guerrillas' bombing of the Havana airport took place when we were already on our flight from Miami to Havana, which took five or six hours in those days. Since the airplanes were piston aircraft and we had already gone beyond the point of no return, we couldn't go back to Miami. We had to continue on, so we landed at a bombed-out terminal.

As we descended into Havana, we saw the demolished airfield where the bomb had hit, but we were young and adventurous so we weren't afraid. When we landed, we tiptoed our way through the smoking rubble and got a cab to the Habana Hilton, Latin America's tallest and largest hotel. Conrad Hilton and his companion, actress Ann Miller; gossip columnist Hedda Hopper; dancer Vera Ellen and ABC network President Leonard Goldenson were among the 300 invited socialites and celebrities who had attended the grand opening in March 1958. The impressive five-story hotel boasted an elegant casino, six restaurants and bars, a huge supper club, convention facilities, an outdoor pool and 630 guest rooms. It was gorgeous.

My friend Pat and I quickly dropped our bags in our room and went to have a drink at the bar. I met a very handsome Cuban lawyer and later, when he took me dancing, he said, "You dance better than Cuban women! Where'd you ever learn to dance?'" I told him about Osea and Willie and we had a glorious two days together in Havana.

Pat and I had made plans to go on to Jamaica, but we only stayed there one day and returned to Havana. The Jamaican men were very aggressive—always saying things like "Missy, meet me around the corner, missy this, missy that"—and we were scared of them. Pat had met somebody in Havana too, so we drank and danced with our new boyfriends for a couple more days before we had to return to the United States.

Castro marched into Havana and took over the city in January of 1959. He set up headquarters for all major diplomatic events at the Habana Hilton in the Castellana Suite, which is now kept as a museum. Osea, Willie and all of us in New York were so happy when Castro took over Havana. We danced in celebration. We loved Cuba, and I've gone back there to visit many times since then.

Years later, after I quit the airlines, married my first husband, Jan, and moved to Saugerties, Osea and Willie came upstate with their two children to visit on many weekends. I would fix everyone a nice dinner on Saturday evening, and during the warmer months, we would sit out on my patio, which was also our driveway, and enjoy each other's company. Osea and I remained friends for 30 years until she died.

Cooking for four on a limited budget and being a responsible tenant (not to mention assuming the role of building supervisor) helped me realize I could care well for myself and for others too. I've stretched into many new leadership roles during my lifetime, but those two experiences laid an early foundation of faith, confidence, belief in myself and the tenacity to accept new challenges.

Others relied upon me and I liked the feeling of taking charge. I might not have become a franchise owner or had the confidence to take on a national leadership role at KFC without first facing these challenges and proving I could prevail.

I became a leader by starting small—preparing one roasted chicken and signing one lease for a third-floor walk-up.

CHAPTER 7

Have a Smile for Everyone You Meet

If your subconscious mind thinks you're happy, it feeds happy thoughts to your conscious mind.

When I was a flight attendant, I always lived in Queens. It was less expensive and I could take the E or F train to Manhattan in 15 minutes.

Moving from Columbus, Ohio to New York City was daunting initially. At first, when I rode the subway, I let others get off ahead of me. But after I missed a couple stops by being so polite, I learned to push my way forward. Riding the New York City subways provided a lesson in being assertive.

I started flying in January, and my roommates and I were "on reserve," which meant we flew when they needed us, and we got five days off a month. I dated a lot of men—not necessarily passengers—and I was never monogamous. I had a lot of boyfriends all over the United States; otherwise, layovers would have been boring. If I flew non-stop from New York to Los Angeles, I'd have a 20-to-24-hour layover in L.A. once I had enough seniority. Before that, I had mainly dated men from Columbus, but now I had boyfriends in California, Kansas City, Pittsburgh and Dayton, where we often had layovers. I enjoyed their company, and all their dinner invitations helped me stay on my very limited budget.

One cold, rainy day in Queens, I rode the Q-33 bus to the airport terminal. I was feeling a little down, a little homesick, when I came across an article in *Reader's Digest* about William James, the great philosopher of the 19th century. He said that if you want to pick yourself up and need to put yourself in a better mood, you can do so by controlling your subconscious mind. Your conscious mind feeds your subconscious mind, which then feeds back to your conscious mind. The article stated that the quickest way to pick yourself up when you're feeling down is to start singing or start whistling.

So, on that cold, rainy day, I began singing on the bus—la, de, da, da, da, da. People looked at me like I was a little crazy, but I didn't care. By the time I got off the bus, I felt better.

This simple trick has worked for me throughout my life.

When I was a young girl, my mother loved to play the piano and we sang together. Here is one of our favorite tunes. The lyrics are a good reminder to change your tune, if you want to change your perspective.

**Have a Smile for Everyone You Meet and
They Will Have a Smile for You**
Lyric by J Keirn Brennan and Paul Cunningham. Music by Bert Rule.

When you're blue and things go wrong with you,
Don't try to share it, grin and bear it,
And your dreams are sure to come true;
When you're sad,
Just make believe you're glad,
And all the world will smile with you.

REFRAIN
Have a smile for ev'ry one you meet,
And ev'ry one will have a smile for you.
Ev'ry mile along life's busy street
Is filled with friendship true.
Each tomorrow
Brings new sorrow,
So why borrow tears?
The thing to do is have a smile
For ev'ry one you meet,
And they will have a smile for you.

When you fear the days because they're drear,
Don't you regret it, just forget it,
And the sun is sure to appear;
Pride and pluck,
Will always bring good luck,
So keep on smiling while you're here.

CHAPTER 8

Impress for Success

*People always watch you and assess how you conduct yourself.
If you don't stand out, they won't know you're there.*

Few young women were chosen to be flight attendants: Only three to five of every 100 applicants were accepted for training. Although I had been offered positions at both TWA and American Airlines, I chose TWA because its planes stopped in Columbus and I could go home easily. The Lockheed Company had a plane called the Constellation—we called it the Connie—and I flew on those for a year and a half before the jets came in. The Jet Age ushered in speed and quieter, smoother travel, as well as an elite era of American power, cultural prowess and technological advances. The number of U.S. airline passengers doubled between 1958 and 1965.

Trans World Airlines (TWA) was one of the Big Four domestic US airlines—the others were American, United and Eastern—and it was owned by Howard Hughes from the 1930s until he gave up control in the 1960s. TWA's previous Kansas City headquarters was supplanted in 1962 by the impressive new TWA Flight Center, a modern international hub designed by the architectural icon Eero Saarinen, at John F. Kennedy International Airport. Over the next few decades, the TWA terminal expanded, then shutdown and later underwent extensive renovations to be transformed into the TWA Hotel, which opened in 2019.

Flight attendants in the 1950s and '60s adhered to an impeccable dress code. Our beautifully tailored, custom-fitted brown and green uniforms were designed by Oleg Cassini. We were required to wear padded bras and girdles—and there were girdle checks to make sure we did—along with brown and white spectator pumps and of course, white gloves.

Revlon's "Love That Red" was our signature lipstick shade and we were permitted to wear only one piece of conservative jewelry. We were forbidden to be married, pregnant or have children, and we could not work past the age of 32, and then we had to quit—practices which should have ended in 1964 when the Civil Rights Age and Sex Discrimination Act became law, but TWA continued them for some time afterwards. We received strict instructions about grooming, hair styling, makeup, posture and how to walk. Our look was polished and glamorous, and we were expected to be polite, friendly, desirable and competent. We wanted to see—and seize—the world and most of us couldn't wait to leave our hometowns and past lives, which we saw as boring in comparison to what the flight attendant lifestyle offered us.

Passenger safety is the real reason flight attendants are on duty—it's not to serve coffee—although we also offered extensive service and meals, more so than flight attendants do today. My training focused on how to serve passengers a sophisticated menu—including Chateaubriand, Lobster Thermidor, martinis and champagne—but the main thrust was emergency training. We learned about each type of plane, the evacuation procedures, where the emergency exits were and how to assist passengers who became ill. Learning to deal with disagreeable passengers and diffuse potentially volatile situations helped me develop my ability to be assertive. But one event that took place early on made me stand out from my co-workers, and my moxie worked to my benefit.

There are bag checks when flight attendants report for duty, and during one bag check, my friend and roommate, Pat, was fired for allegedly having stolen the tea bags that were found in her suitcase. Helen Fugate, who was the person in charge of flight attendants, was the one who fired Pat.

"Pat, you come with me," I said. "We're going to see Miss Fugate."

Certain stations didn't replenish the supplies on the planes and Pittsburgh was one of them. I told Miss Fugate that

Pat was merely being exemplary by carrying tea bags with her. She wasn't stealing them—she wanted to make sure her service stations were fully stocked.

Pat got her job back.

I must have stood out in Helen Fugate's mind because she called me into her office six months later.

"I want to offer you a position as Supervisor of Flight Attendants," said Miss Fugate.

"But you have women who are 28 or 29—much older than I am—and more experienced than me," I protested. "They should have that position. I've only flown a year and a half."

But Helen Fugate said, "You're the best at what you do. You can do it."

I accepted, and at age 21, I became the youngest-ever supervisor of TWA flight attendants.

However, there was no training program for the job, so I had no way of knowing what I was supposed to do. At the LaGuardia Airport TWA offices, I went through drawers, reading whatever I could, to train myself. It didn't give me a lot of confidence, especially because I was supervising older women. As a supervisor, I only got to fly when I had to check runs, and when I did fly, I was not serving passengers. I worked as supervisor for six months until I asked Miss Fugate for a meeting.

"I can do better, financially, as a flight attendant and I miss flying," I told her. "I enjoy working with the passengers more than being a supervisor. I want to be a flight attendant again."

She wasn't happy about my request, but she understood and approved it.

I never would have been tapped for this supervisory position—and especially not at such a young age—if I hadn't made a strong first impression on Helen Fugate. Honesty, integrity and a willingness to (politely) bring unfair or ineffective policies to the attention of management speak volumes about an employee's initiative, trustworthiness and commitment to customer service. Decades later, when I owned my Kentucky Fried Chicken franchises, I looked for similar

DARLENE L. PFEIFFER

qualities in the people I hired to work for me.

First impressions count and so do all the little things you do—and don't do—on a daily basis. Pay attention to details as they count for more than most people realize. Combined, these attributes can add up to more responsibility, more pay and the deeper satisfaction that comes from striving to be an exemplary person.

Always try to make a good first impression, but don't stop there. Every minute offers a new opportunity to improve how others see you. Make sure your actions reflect your good intentions.

CHAPTER 9

Stand Your Ground

Asserting authority and taking a stand are natural to some people, but others find it difficult to insist people adhere to established policies. Even if the person you're confronting is a revered public figure, learning to uphold principles is a vital leadership quality.

I've interacted with many famous people and worked closely with some of them. Some are well known to millions, while others are local heroes.

I've never felt famous people deserve special consideration just because they're public figures. When anyone does something to negatively impact the wellbeing of others—especially when it's your job to make sure others are safe, comfortable and treated fairly—then you have to step up and do the right thing.

When I was a TWA flight attendant, we had many celebrities and influential people who were used to getting their own way on our flights. Air travel was still a novelty for most people and tickets were expensive, so many of our passengers were among the elite. Flight attendants rotated schedules between first-class and coach, so even when I was a senior flight attendant, I sometimes served in the back of the plane. One day, a new flight attendant came to the back, crying.

"Mary, what's wrong?" I asked her.

"Jack Parr just called me a bitch," she sobbed.

"What happened?"

"He wanted a certain seat and I couldn't give it to him. It was already taken by someone else."

I handed Mary a tissue and told her to compose herself. Then I marched right up the aisle to Parr, who was the host of *The Tonight Show* and often traveled on TWA.

"Mr. Parr, we have nothing to do with seating. If you want to change your seat, you'll have to walk outside, talk to a ticket agent and ask them to change it. We cannot change it."

"But I always sit in 2A," he protested, sounding like a spoiled child.

"It's not our fault and we cannot change your seat," I said. "And furthermore, if you cannot treat all of us with respect, or if I hear any further foul language from you, you'll have to get off the plane. Please take your seat or get off the plane. The choice is yours."

He sat down and shut up.

Another time, two members of The Rat Pack, Frank Sinatra and Peter Lawford, were on my flight. We were taking off and the plane was still climbing when Sinatra's bodyguard got out of his seat to rummage around in the overhead compartment. Sinatra, who had released his 14th studio album, *Come Fly With Me*, in January 1958, was one of the most famous singers in the world and the epitome of the Jet Set.

"Sir! You'll have to sit down," I told his bodyguard.

"But Mr. Sinatra wants something out of his bag."

"Well, Mr. Sinatra is going to have to wait because you have to sit down and fasten your seat belt. It's against Federal Aviation Administration rules to be out of your seat during takeoff."

He immediately sat down.

Being a flight attendant was good training for me. I learned to deal with all kinds of people and wasn't shy about insisting my passengers adhere to the rules. These early experiences laid the foundation for my management style when I became a successful businesswoman a decade or so later.

CHAPTER 10

Who Are You?

It isn't always easy to admit you have made a mistake or do not know something. Being honest demands confidence, humility, even a touch of humor—all of which can serve you well and become strengths.

One reason I loved being a TWA flight attendant was we had great passengers, including celebrities like Eleanor Roosevelt, Frank Sinatra, Margaret Meade, Ed Sullivan, Mitch Miller, Vince Lombardi and the entire Yankees team. One day I learned Bishop Fulton Sheen, one of the first televangelists and a renowned theologian, would be seated in first class on my flight.

My mother and Aunt Eloise loved listening to him on the radio and then watching *Life Is Worth Living* and his other inspirational TV shows, but not being Catholic, I wasn't sure how to address him. I saw two nuns dressed in habits who had just gotten on my flight, so I asked them.

"Call him Monsignor Sheen," they said.

"Would you care for a cocktail, Monsignor Sheen? Would you like some hors d'oeuvres, Monsignor Sheen?"

The call button buzzed: It was the two nuns summoning me to their seats.

"We're so sorry, he's been elevated to Bishop. We're so sorry."

I was embarrassed but learned an important lesson: Even trusted authority figures can be wrong. I went right over to him and knelt down to speak with him so nearby passengers wouldn't hear.

"I don't know if you've noticed," I said, "but I've been addressing you as Monsignor. I'm so sorry, Bishop Sheen."

He took my hand, patted it, looked kindly into my eyes and said, "My dear, you could call me anything you want to."

I felt his forgiveness, as well as his grace.

"By the way," he added, "I'm filming my next television show here in Chicago. Why don't you come by the studio to watch us film it?"

He had a compelling presence on television, all the more remarkable because his show featured him simply speaking into the camera to share the teachings of the Bible and respond to viewer letters. Twice honored with Emmy Awards for Most Outstanding Television Personality, he was featured on the cover of *Time* magazine and his show attracted as many as 30 million viewers each week.

"Oh, Bishop Sheen, what an honor!" I said. "I enjoy watching your program and would love to attend but unfortunately I'm doing a turnaround flight right back to New York after we land at O'Hare. If I didn't have to work, I would definitely be there. Thank you for the invitation."

Another time, Ed Sullivan and his wife boarded our plane in Las Vegas and I heard from others he was very personable. As the Sullivans made their way to their seats, I took his hat and coat, and Ed said, "You're a beautiful young lady. I hope this flight is better than the last one. We couldn't leave and were delayed a couple of hours."

It seems every time he flew with TWA, he had a bad experience. I was determined to help make this flight a good one.

"No, Mr. Sullivan, this flight will be your best one yet."

We took off, but soon an announcement came over the loudspeaker: there was a mechanical problem. The pilot flew over the desert, dumped fuel and took the plane back to land in Las Vegas. As passengers were getting off the plane, Mr. Sullivan neglected to grab his hat. I handed it to him, saying, "You'd better take this with you in case we board a different plane when we fly out again."

We were delayed two hours. When you are a flight attendant, you have no control over the weather or the plane. You learn to be humble about it and you say you're sorry a lot, which became a habit I had to break later in life.

When Mr. Sullivan and his wife got back on the plane,

DREAM BIG, ADD MOXIE

I apologized for our delay and said, "I'm sorry we didn't live up to your expectations of TWA. I promised you a good experience."

He was understanding and as he and his wife got settled into their seats, I told him how much my mother loved his television program.

"She watches your show every week," I said. "In fact, she's coming from Columbus, Ohio to visit me this weekend in New York, and she'll be so thrilled to hear I met you."

"Great, that's wonderful," Mr. Sullivan said. "Bring her down to the show! Give me your name and I'll have seats for you and your mother. And," he added, "thank you for making this my best TWA experience."

On the day of *The Ed Sullivan Show*, I went to the ticket booth when we arrived at the theater and said, "I'm not sure if Mr. Sullivan remembered, but he said he would leave tickets for me and my mother."

"Oh yes," said the man. "Mr. Sullivan spoke very highly of you and left two tickets for you. You'll be seated in Row 2 for the live broadcast of the show."

Before we went on the air, Ed came down to say hello to my mother and invited us both to come up on stage with him.

Ed Sullivan, Darlene, her mother 1964.

He was such a sweet, gracious man and he made a big fuss over Mom. I still have a picture of the two of us with him—in it, he is shaking hands with my mother, who has a huge smile on her face.

That October 25, 1964 show was the debut of the Rolling Stones' first visit to America, but to me, they looked like a motley crew. Their hair was long and dirty and they wore sweatshirts—they were definitely not what I considered to be handsome young men. I didn't think they were going to be great stars but guess what? They're still around and that appearance kicked off more than a half century of huge success for them.

My mother never forgot that day. She often told people about how she spent an afternoon with one of the most famous men in America—and she didn't mean Mick Jagger!

I was never a big sports fan, but everyone knew the Yankees were top stars in Major League Baseball: They played eight World Series from 1950 to 1959 and won six of them.

In the early 1960s, the entire Yankees team was onboard one of my flights and the buzz among the passengers was palpable.

At the time I was dating Ray, a New York City lawyer who lived catty-corner from the Waldorf-Astoria in the same rent-controlled building as my Aunt Vera. Ray and I met on a Sunday evening flight to Dayton when he ordered a cocktail and I sold him some miniature bottles of alcohol before the flight ended, having tipped him off about Ohio's Blue Laws, which prevented sales of alcohol on Sundays. With that, Ray and I started a very long romance and friendship. He was handsome, smart and domineering, and we were very good friends.

I knew that Ray, his family and an elderly family friend who lived in Bridgeport, Connecticut, would be impressed when I told them I'd had the Yankees on my flight.

But I had a problem: I didn't know any of the Yankees team members. I decided to find out who was on board and went over to a handsome blond man who was flirting with me. He put his hands in the back of his head and flexed his muscles at me.

"I'm so thrilled to have you Yankees on board, but I don't know who any of you are," I said. "What's your name?"

All his teammates laughed at me and started teasing him, 'She doesn't know your name!'

"I'm Mickey Mantle," he said, very boastfully.

My innocent follow-up question to America's most favorite Yankee brought even more laughter from everyone who heard me ask, "And what do you do?"

Mantle, who had taken over center field in 1952 after Joe DiMaggio retired, was one of the team's most valuable players and everyone—everyone but me—knew who he was. He had a huge ego and was used to people bowing down before him because of all the national attention he received. That day he was miffed by my questions but still managed to be friendly, despite his injured pride over my ignorance.

Before they got off the plane, all of the famous Yankees signed a baseball which I gave to Ray for his parents' friend. Not long after that, I dated Eli Grba, who pitched for the Yankees for a couple of years until he was traded to the Los Angeles Angels.

I've never been afraid to ask questions, apologize or admit I've made a mistake. How else are you going to learn? Most people are happy to answer questions about themselves and, if they aren't, that gives you another answer about their character, their pride or their insecurities.

Learning is an asset and what you witness in the process can be quite revealing—not only about yourself but about others. Those who act like, or think, they know everything are often quite wrong. Humility is an admirable quality.

CHAPTER 11

Mentor: Jake Gottlieb
Give Someone Else a Boost

All of us are clawing our way up a mountain—in our lives and in our careers. We're trying to succeed at goals that are important to us, while other people often depend upon us to help and take care of them as we're striving to get to the top. We all need someone to give us a boost.

I met Jake Gottlieb around 1960 because of my desire to get tickets to the most sought-after show in Las Vegas. My boyfriend, Jack, and I had never been to Vegas and we were planning to go there for a long weekend. I had tried, unsuccessfully, to get tickets to see Sammy Davis, Jr., Dean Martin, Frank Sinatra, Joey Bishop and Peter Lawford—The Rat Pack—when my roommate and fellow flight attendant, Colleen, told me to go see Dave Goldstein, the pit boss at the Dunes Hotel.

"Maybe Dave can get you tickets. Go see him when you arrive and tell him I sent you," said Colleen.

I arrived in Vegas three hours ahead of Jack, went to the Dunes Hotel and approached a woman seated high on a chair overlooking the scene.

"Could you please tell me where Dave Goldstein is?" I asked her.

"He's over there. In the pit," she replied.

I walked away and started looking for a hole in the floor or a BBQ pit but didn't see anything that looked like a pit. I went back to the woman.

"Excuse me, ma'am. Could you just tell me what a pit looks like?"

I later learned "pit" was the term for the floor of the casino. The pit is encased by all the gaming tables where the dealers stand and the pit boss stands above it all to monitor the action.

The woman shot me an exasperated look and scanned the upper level of the room. "There he is," she said, pointing at a man standing on the mezzanine floor, intent on watching everything happening below him on the casino floor.

"Hello, Dave, nice to meet you," I told him. "I'm Darlene Large and Colleen Finn is my roommate. Colleen told me perhaps you could help me get tickets to see the Rat Pack."

"Is she a dancer here?" he asked me.

"No, she's my friend. We're both flight attendants," I replied.

"Oh, OK. Come with me." He led me over to the cocktail lounge off the casino and told me to wait.

I took a seat and after a few moments, Dave returned with another handsome, middle-aged man.

"Jake, I want you to meet Darlene," Dave said.

I had no idea who Jake was and even to this day, never understood why Dave brought the owner of the Dunes over to meet me. But fate dealt me a good hand with that introduction.

Jake sat down across the table from me and greeted me warmly, "Hi, honey." After we shared a few minutes of friendly conversation, he asked me where I was staying.

"I'm staying at the Thunderbird."

"The Thunderbird? Why are you staying at that fire trap?! Come over here to the Dunes. You can stay here as my guest."

Dave quickly interrupted Jake and spoke up, with some exasperation. "She has her boyfriend with her, Mr. Gottlieb," he said.

"Well, I don't care," Jake replied, looking at me. "Bring your boyfriend too."

"Let me talk to Jack," I said, hesitant to decide without consulting him.

"OK," Jake said, "and now what show do you want to see?"

I told Jake I'd like to see the Rat Pack. Rat Pack tickets were the most coveted in Vegas; most people had to wait a month to secure them, and I had been trying, unsuccessfully, to buy a couple of them.

Jake picked up a nearby phone and called the Sands, where the Rat Pack was headlining. "We need two tickets for the Rat Pack for tomorrow night."

"When you get there tomorrow night, ask for Yale Cohen and he'll take care of you," Jake said after he hung up the phone.

And that was that. I thanked Jake and left the casino. When Jack arrived later that night, I told him about Jake's offer and how nice he had been to me, and then asked him, "Do you think it's OK if we take him up on his offer to stay at the Dunes?"

"Sure, honey," Jack said.

So I called Jake the next morning to say Jack and I would be delighted to accept his generous offer to be his guests at the Dunes. I thanked him again for getting us tickets to see the Rat Pack.

When the Dunes debuted in 1955—at the cost of $3.5 million—it was designed in an Arabian Desert theme. A 35-foot-tall fiberglass sultan stood with arms akimbo above its main entrance. Nicknamed "the Miracle in the Desert," the Dunes was the first hotel-casino visitors saw when arriving by car from southern California, and it was the 10th resort to occupy the famous Strip. It had a 90-foot V-shaped swimming pool and Hollywood stars and other top performers headlined shows in its Arabian Room, which was the size of a full Broadway theater.

Jake bought the Dunes in 1956, and by 1965 had added a 24-story hotel tower (the tallest building in Nevada at the time) along with 800 new guest rooms, an 18-hole, par-72 golf course and the Top O' the Strip restaurant and lounge and a new exhibition/convention hall—all of which enhanced the Dunes' stature as a modern showpiece and one of the best destinations in Las Vegas. Minsky's Follies—featuring the first bare-breasted showgirls in Vegas—caused a profitable controversy, selling a record 16,000 tickets in one week, and after that, the showroom was used for the Casino de Paris, the first music hall to be imported from France with its original cast.

Gourmet dining arrived on the Strip when the Dunes opened the Sultan's Table restaurant. It featured a delectable assortment of hors d'oeuvres like Terrine de Foie Grax aux Truffles, Lobster Bisque and Escargots de Bourgogne and two of my favorite entrées, Long Island Duckling à l'Orange and Prime Filet Mignon aux Champignons. The Diner's Club called it "America's finest and most beautiful new restaurant" when it opened, and by December of 1965, it was the only Las Vegas restaurant named on *Esquire* magazine's Gourmet Feast list.

Our entire weekend was impressive, and it seemed Jack and I ran into Jake every time we entered the Dunes' lobby.

"What are you kids doing today?" he asked the first time he saw us.

When we said we had no special plans, Jake said, "Be my guest tonight for dinner at the Sultan's Table."

The next day, the same thing happened. There was Jake in the lobby again, asking us what our plans were for the evening, and when we replied we had nothing planned, he invited us to be his guests, this time for an evening show in the theater.

When the end of our stay rolled around on Sunday, I asked Jack, "Why do you think he's doing all this? He has all the most beautiful women here."

Every girl who worked in Vegas was tall and gorgeous. Many had breast implants and performed topless. They wore huge, beautiful headdresses and stunning gowns, and were so nice-looking on stage. I felt attractive in a normal kind of way, but I certainly wasn't glamorous like these women. I'd never seen anyone like them.

"I think he likes you, Darlene," Jack said.

Before we left Vegas that weekend, Jake gave me his personal number in Chicago, so when I returned to New York, I called to thank him for the weekend. A few weeks later, when one of my other boyfriends—Ray, the lawyer—was going to Vegas, I had the audacity to call Jake again—this time to request a favor.

"Do you think you could get Ray tickets to a show or two?"

"Sure, honey. I'll be glad to. Just tell him to ask for me at the Dunes and I'll make sure he's taken care of," said Jake. Unbeknownst to me, Jake also fixed Ray up with a prostitute. Later he told me, "I figured I'd get his mind off you."

The next time I saw Jake, he was a passenger on my flight and gave me a wad of bills before deplaning in Chicago. When I looked at it, I was breathless. It was three $100 bills. I had never seen that much money before.

"Here," he said with a smile, "take this and don't argue with me."

Twenty minutes later when my boyfriend, Ray, came onto that same Chicago flight, I dragged him back to the galley, shut the curtain and said, "You'll never believe what Mr. Gottlieb just gave me!" and showed him the money. We were talking excitedly about it when I happened to look out the galley curtains to see Jake approaching us. I shut the curtain quickly and stepped out into the aisle again so Jake wouldn't see Ray hidden in there.

"Mr. Gottlieb, may I help you?"

"I think I left my hat when I got off the plane," he said.

I looked around for it but there wasn't any hat—he told me later it was a lie, just an excuse to see me again—but before Jake got off the plane again, I said, "My mother needs a new hot water heater and the money you gave me will buy it for her. Thank you so much! I really appreciate it!"

He just smiled at me and walked down the stairs to leave.

Eventually, I learned Jake always had a pocket full of $100 bills and freely distributed tips to waiters, airport gate agents, limo drivers and the people who worked on the ground at the airport.

Another time, just before the holidays, Jake was on my flight to Vegas and asked me when I would be coming back again. I told him the date and he said, "Well, when you get in, ask the gate agent for a package. I'm going to leave something for you."

A few days later when I flew back into Vegas, I asked the gate agent if Mr. Gottlieb had left a package for me. He looked at me like I was dirt.

"I doubt he'd leave a package for *you*!"

Just then Rudy the bell captain came towards us, pulling a cart piled high with beautifully wrapped packages. I had never received so many presents from anyone before, and when I opened them later at home, I found purses, stockings, clothes, perfume, you name it.

When the gate agent came onto the plane before we began boarding passengers, I said, "I told you Mr. Gottlieb had something for me."

"I'm so sorry, Miss Large. Please forgive me," he said, acknowledging how he had misjudged my status.

Jake frequently traveled on my flights to and from Las Vegas, as often as once a week for quite a while, and we dated for the next few years. Sometimes he flew to New York to spend time with me, and thanks to his generosity and impeccable good taste, I learned to appreciate many of the finer things in life.

Whenever I landed in Vegas after working my flight, I would change in the galley from my uniform into fancy evening wear before I floated down the stairs of the plane. A waiting stretch limo whisked me away to meet Jake at the Sultan's Table for dinner and an evening out. An expensive bottle of Dom Perignon champagne would be chilled and waiting for me and the Captain at the Sultan's Table always joined me in finishing the bottle. After dinner, I often enjoyed Coffee Diablo, which featured a flaming orange peel descending into the rich brew—one of my girlfriends said, "Be sure to take your fire extinguisher if you're meeting Darlene."

About a year after we started dating, Jake said, "I want to get a car for you."

I didn't have a car because I lived in Queens so I didn't need one.

"Why would I want a car?"

"Nonsense. I'm going to send a Cadillac to you."

"I don't want a Cadillac. It's just too much. It's the finest car available!"

"Well, honey, what do you want?"

I stuttered a little, and said hesitantly, "Well, how about a Pontiac?"

I was making an effort to suggest a car that was less expensive, less flashy than a Cadillac.

Within a week, someone drove a beautiful new turquoise Pontiac Bonneville to Queens, parked it in front of my apartment, knocked on my door and handed me the keys. The next year, Jake gave me a brand-new Cadillac and I've always had a Cadillac ever since. Think of it: me at age 23 with a brand-new Bonneville and the next year, at 24, the owner of my first Cadillac.

A while into our relationship, Jake gave me a magnificent five-carat pear-shaped diamond ring. I loved it and wore it constantly. On one of my flights, my supervisor called me into her office. Georgina sternly said, "You know the regulations, Darlene. You can only wear one piece of conservative jewelry when you're working."

The diamond was breathtaking. Few people in the world had a ring like that, let alone a flight attendant. Jake had to give me a ring to match—even upstage—his friends' girlfriends' jewelry, and my ring was stunning.

"Well, come out to the trunk of my car if you think this is not conservative," I said. "I'll show you one that is truly not conservative, one that's even bigger."

I was bluffing—there wasn't any other jewelry in the trunk of my car. Even though I knew my ring was not conservative, I wore it because it reminded me of Jake and made me happy.

It was love at first sight for us, and Jake never stopped loving me, no matter how many other men I dated, not even after I got married. Looking back, he saw things in me—my drive, my moxie, my tenacity, my strength of conviction—before I fully realized those qualities in myself. Once, when I was dating an architect, I lost a nice diamond earring from a set Jake had given to me. All Jake said when I told him was, "I hope he didn't swallow it!" He never got angry like a lot of men would.

Jake's bodyguard, Angie, brought me a tiny, black toy poodle. It was only about two pounds and fit into Angie's palm. I named it "JG" after Jake. I loved that poodle so much because she was a gift from Jake. I don't know how that dog knew she belonged to me from the very first moment we met, but that's the way it was. JG was quite protective of me and, at just two months old, she would lift her lip, expose her teeth and growl at anyone who approached us. I was JG's precious cargo and she was my bodyguard. JG never let anyone come near me without defending me.

At the end of 1960, Jake received a coveted invitation to attend the Swearing-In Ceremony and all the festivities for John F. Kennedy's inauguration on January 20, 1961. I was thrilled when he asked me to accompany him! Frank Sinatra and Peter Lawford were hosting a ball at the D.C. Armory on the eve of Inauguration Day—it was sure to be one of the biggest parties ever held in Washington, D.C.—and we were also invited to attend a second ball that night hosted by JFK's father, Joseph Kennedy. On Inauguration Day, following the swearing-in ceremonies for the youngest American President,

Darlene with J.G., a gift from Jake. Jackson Heights, NY, circa 1965.

Jake and I planned to enjoy the parade procession to the White House and attend several evening balls. I had all my outfits laid out and was excited to imagine being that close to JFK and Jackie.

But shortly before we were set to leave for D.C., I became violently ill. I didn't know what was wrong with me. A doctor made a house call to see me and told me I just had a bad flu. My mother was due to come stay with me, and even though Ray and I were on the outs because I was dating Jake, I called him to ask a favor.

"I'm very sick and my mother is flying into New York from Columbus this evening," I told him. "Could you please meet her at the airport and bring her to my apartment?"

When Ray arrived at my place with my mother, he took one look at me and called the doctor.

"Get your ass over here," he barked into the phone. "I'm an attorney and I am going to sue you. This woman is dying!"

The doctor called an ambulance. When it arrived, the drivers couldn't get their stretcher up to my third-floor apartment. The ambulance drivers put me on a kitchen chair, and I held on for dear life as they carried me down three very narrow flights of stairs. I was admitted to the hospital and diagnosed with a ruptured appendix. I underwent emergency surgery then and there.

My mother called Jake the next morning to let him know my condition and he said, "I want her to have private care and a nurse with her at all times when you're not there. She can't be left alone." He hired a nurse who worked at St. Claire's Hospital to care for me each night from 8:00 p.m. until 8:00 a.m., and every day he sent a taxi for my mother so she could visit me in the hospital. Ray sent me flowers from the finest florist in New York City; Jake sent me gorgeous bouquets as well. It was the battle of the bouquets, and I asked my mother to hide Jake's bouquets when Ray came to visit me.

After three weeks in the hospital, I was finally discharged though I was still quite ill and weak. I decided my mother, my dog JG and I would fly to Vegas so I could fully recuperate there. I could barely move. Jake paid for the whole thing as well as for a private duty nurse who came in each night for weeks. I couldn't walk without assistance and the nurse was a lifesaver. I lost three months of work because the peritonitis had traveled throughout my body. Today, antibiotics and penicillin have diminished the damaging effects of peritonitis, but in those days, a ruptured appendix often led to death.

While I was convalescing in Vegas for a month, I completely ignored Ray. I didn't tell him I was leaving New York and I never called him while I was away. Ray and I were open about the fact we were both dating others, but he was jealous and I just didn't have the energy or desire to deal with him.

On my flight back to New York from Vegas, a pilot friend told me Ray had gotten married. I had known he was dating someone else, but I was shocked he'd married her while I was gone. I didn't contact him when I returned to the East Coast.

By then I was dating Jan, among many other boyfriends, and still seeing Jake occasionally, but I was feeling lonely. My two roommates, who were also flight attendants, had both gotten married and I was living alone.

Jake said, "Don't go to the bother of getting more roommates," and helped me pay for my apartment, but I was lonely alone in my apartment. When I went to visit Jake in Vegas, I was always waiting around for him.

Though I felt glamorous being in Vegas, I usually sat alone at the Sultan's Table while Jake was working. Frank Sinatra was often seated at the table next to mine with his new wife and their friends. Hollywood directors frequently asked me, "Would you like to be in the movies, honey?" but I never wanted to do that.

One night, I was seated at the Sultan's Table again, waiting for Jake to have dinner with me, when he came over to ask me a question.

"Would you mind having dinner with Cary Grant?"

Cary Grant was one of Hollywood's most debonair classic

leading men. He was famous for his roles in several acclaimed films directed by Alfred Hitchcock, as well as films in which he starred with Irene Dunne, Katherine Hepburn, Jimmy Stewart, Ingrid Bergman, Doris Day and Audrey Hepburn.

"No," I told Jake, "that would be fine." I didn't get really excited, because thank God I was a flight attendant and was used to being around celebrities. Cary was waiting for his girlfriend to arrive and the two of us spent a pleasant evening talking. He was a lovely man and a charming dinner companion.

In about 1963 or 1964, I received a subpoena to appear for a Grand Jury hearing at the United States Internal Revenue Service office. The notice said they were investigating Jake, so I called him immediately.

"I'll have an attorney get in touch with you," he said.

My brief conversation with that attorney, who was supposedly friendly, scared me as much as going up against the IRS people.

"Watch what you say," he warned me. "You could lose your job with TWA. I'm telling you lady, you watch yourself."

On the day of the hearing, I took two subway trains from Queens to the Federal Court House in Brooklyn. You cannot have an attorney present with you when you appear at a Grand Jury hearing and when I arrived at the courthouse, I still had no idea why I had been subpoenaed. The prospect of being grilled on the witness stand for a couple of hours was very frightening, especially without legal counsel present. But there I was—and it became immediately clear through the line of questioning that things were very serious.

"Miss Large, I understand you are a flight attendant for TWA. Is that correct?"

"Yes, I began flying in January of 1958."

"Miss Large, please tell us when you first met Jake Gottlieb."

I knew instinctively it was best to say as little as possible, to simply answer the questions and offer little more unless pressed for additional details.

"It was 1960. I went to Vegas with my boyfriend and we stayed at the Dunes."

"Please tell the court what ensued."

"Mr. Gottlieb was kind enough to get us tickets to see the Rat Pack at the Sands Hotel," I replied. "We were quite excited. It was a wonderful show."

"And when did you next see Mr. Gottlieb, Miss Large?"

I decided against saying Jake had invited us to be his guests at the Dunes—and comped our dinners at the Sultan's Table that weekend—and replied, "He was a passenger on my flight from Chicago to Las Vegas."

"And what did he do to make himself stand out in your memory?"

I wasn't about to tell them Jake had given me a $300 cash tip, so I said, "He was an attractive, well-spoken man and he came back onto my flight after deplaning. He thought he had left his hat behind and we chatted for a moment or two while I looked for it. He was mistaken. There was no hat on board that belonged to him."

"How often did Mr. Gottlieb fly on TWA?"

"About once a week I believe. He wasn't always on my flights as I am scheduled to work on routes throughout the United States."

"Please describe your relationship with Mr. Gottlieb."

"We were friendly right from the beginning and began to date on a regular basis shortly after we met."

"How often do you see Mr. Gottlieb now?"

"It varies, but I'd say once or twice a month."

"How does he treat you, Miss Large?"

"Jake is wonderful to me. He is a very kind, charming, generous person. He is very kind to my mother as well."

"How do you spend your time when you are in Las Vegas?"

"When I fly into Vegas, I meet Jake for dinner at the Sultan's Table."

This experienced, middle-aged federal investigator was

trying to catch me in something, but what? As he kept drilling down, drilling down, drilling down, asking me increasingly detailed questions, I started to lead him on just a tiny bit. Near the end of my time on the witness stand, he asked, "Miss Large, when you see Mr. Gottlieb, does he ever give you anything to give to anybody?"

"Yes, he does."

"Does he do it frequently?"

I was seeing Jake on flight layovers once a week or so at that time. "Yes, maybe once a month or so," I replied.

"Tell me, Miss Large, what does he give you?"

I paused for a moment. "He gives me See's Candies to take to my mother," I said. "You can't get them anywhere else and she loves them."

With that, the investigator revealed his exasperation and said, "That's all the questions I have for you, Miss Large. You may step down now."

Later, I realized the federal investigator had been trying to prove Jake was taking money out of Las Vegas and giving it to someone elsewhere—and the authorities suspected I was a courier—but that day, my stint on the witness stand solidified something I already knew: You always have to be sharp and you always have to have a story.

Sometimes Jake would call me and say, "Maybe your baby will be in New York this weekend," and then he'd call later to say he couldn't make it.

One evening when we were out on the town together, I was wearing the gorgeous five-carat, pear-shaped diamond he had given me.

"You know, Jake, if I put this ring down on the curb and leave it there, someone will pick it up within minutes and it will be gone," I said. "And that's what's going to happen to me." So, I gave him warning: "If you don't spend more time with me, I'm going to be gone . . ."

I had been dating one of my boyfriends, Jan, who was a casket distributor from Columbus, Ohio, for about seven years by then, but I didn't see him often.

On November 9, 1965, on a TWA flight coming into JFK, I made my usual announcement: "Passengers, if you look out the windows on the left side of the plane, you'll see all the lights of Manhattan and the Wall Street area. It's a beautiful clear night and we will be landing shortly. Enjoy your time in New York City."

But as I was walking back to my seat in the galley, a passenger stopped me and said, "All the lights below just went out. What happened?"

I looked out the window and, sure enough, all I could see was darkness below.

"I don't know. I'll go ask the Captain."

All the lights in New York City—and all along the entire East Coast—had indeed gone out. Nobody knew what had happened. Our plane lost all radio communication with the air traffic control tower. We circled in a holding pattern for three hours before we were finally able to land at Newark, and then had to get rides to take us to our cars at JFK so we could get home.

When I called Jan to tell him about my harrowing experience, he said, "Darlene, why don't you quit flying?"

In those days, quite a few planes did go down. One TWA flight collided with another over New York. Two planes had recently crashed into the Grand Canyon. And now this.

I started thinking maybe my time was up.

That blackout became a huge turning point in my life: Jan and I decided to get married right away. Before the 1964 Civil Rights Act became law, if you got married, you had to quit working for the airlines, so I put in my notice.

The weekend before Jan and I got married, Jake called me. "What would you think if I told you your baby was coming to New York this weekend?"

I said, "What would you think if I told you your baby was getting married this weekend?"

That's how I broke the news to him.

DARLENE L. PFEIFFER

Jan and I got married on November 23, 1965 in Columbus. My mother refused to come to my wedding because she didn't like Jan and thought I should be with Jake.

She called Jake, crying.

"Don't worry, Mom, she'll get rid of that bum," Jake said, and accepted it.

My Aunt Gladys and Uncle Bob were the only members of my family who attended, along with Jan's parents. We returned to New York—Jan's office and casket warehouse were both in Catskill—and moved into our new home in Saugerties, which was known then as "the Garden City of America." I thought that sounded nice.

As a newlywed, I was bored to tears with staying home all day, but by the summertime, I got involved in furnishing our house, even though we had very little money. I hatched a practical plan to sell the chinchilla jacket Jake had given me as a gift when we were dating. I took it to Shabes Furriers in Manhattan, where Jake had purchased all my furs. They knew him well.

On my way out the door, I told the store owner, "Don't tell Jake I'm returning it."

First fur stole – a gift from Jake. Mid 1960s.

Of course the store owner called Jake as soon as I left the store, and Jake called me immediately. People were very loyal to Jake and weren't going to do anything behind his back.

"You are not going to return that chinchilla jacket," Jake said. "Why would you do that?"

"Because eight hundred dollars would furnish my whole house with carpeting. I can use carpeting more than a chinchilla jacket," I said.

"No, you keep your jacket. Come out here and we'll pick out your carpet together," he said.

My husband Jan knew what I was doing and was in favor of it—he figured he had me and Jake didn't, plus we would get free carpeting for our home.

"OK," I said.

Jake flew me to Los Angeles and when I arrived, I learned he had contacted the man who helped him furnish his new Dunes renovation project. True to his word, Jake paid for all the carpeting, but that wasn't all he bought for my new home over the next two days. I had measured all the rooms for the carpet, so Jake's contact in LA helped us figure out what I needed to outfit my entire home. Jake helped me select two sofas and coffee tables for the den and the living room, kitchen table and chairs, bedroom furniture, lamps, drapes—everything, even pictures for the walls—and then shipped it all to New York. Everything was top-of-the-line and beautiful.

I had just dropped Jake to marry someone else, but he said, "I understand, honey," and treated me like nothing had happened. Most men would have been furious—ranting "after all I've done for you and for your mother"—but not Jake. He was always so sweet to me and our relationship was unbelievable. He changed my life forever.

When I went into the franchise business and wanted to buy my first Kentucky Fried Chicken property, Jake loaned me $40,000 to make a down payment on the land, and have the collateral needed to get a bank loan for equipment—and I paid him back. And when my daughter, Bevy, came to live with me in 1970 after her mother, Nancy, died of breast cancer, Jake wanted to meet her. He flew the two of us out to visit him and bought her a beautiful collection of dresses. He made sure my mother and Bevy and I had wonderful times on a few occasions when we were his guests at the Dunes and at the Sultan's Table in Vegas.

People ask me, "What was so special about him?" and I can only say, "Everything was special about him."

Everyone who met Jake seemed to have a sweet story to tell about him and his generosity. A few years ago, Paul DeLisio, my longtime companion and life partner, relayed a conversation he'd had with a local doctor. While he was a young intern from South Africa at The Mayo Clinic in Minneapolis, this doctor met a wonderful man. The man suggested that once the young intern became a doctor, he should accept a position as his personal physician.

"I'd like to hire you for fifty thousand dollars a year to be my personal physician at the Mayo Clinic, where I always go for regular checkups and routine tests," the man said to him. "And I'll buy you a house. Come to Vegas and visit me at the Dunes. We'll talk it over."

The doctor declined the job offer because he wanted to continue on his career path at the Mayo Clinic. "I don't ever want to be owned by anybody. I'm a very independent guy," he told Paul. But he never forgot the man's generous offer and the two stayed in touch over the years. Whenever the man came to the Mayo Clinic, he asked the young doctor who the best specialists were and who he should see. He treated the doctor really well, even when he was only a resident, and gave him money and a condo. They became very good friends and the doctor became a renowned surgeon, working for many years at The Mayo Clinic before moving to Upstate New York.

Then, the surgeon added, "He always had his bodyguard, Angie, with him." Since he had already mentioned the Dunes Hotel, Paul thought it had to be Jake.

"Was this man's name Jake Gottlieb?" Paul asked him.

"What? Did you know him too?"

"I know someone who knew him," Paul responded.

"Really?"

"Yes, a dear friend of mine knew him very well," Paul said. "Let me check with her and I'll find out if it's OK to tell you her name."

When Paul told me he had just met somebody who knew Jake, I said, "Oh my God!" I couldn't believe it and soon Paul introduced me to the doctor who had met Jake in Rochester, Minnesota so many years ago.

It really was quite unusual to sit and talk with this surgeon—now retired and living near me in New York—and share remembrances of our experiences with Jake from 50 years ago. Jake made such an impression on this man, and on me, when we were both young.

As my surgeon friend said to me, "If someone is an extraordinary human being in your life, you never forget them."

Just before Jake died in 1972, I was determined to see him one last time. He was quite ill and I knew he didn't have long to live. I flew to Minneapolis with my little dog JG and my cousin Sue. Shortly after I checked into my hotel room near the hospital, I heard thunderous footsteps like a giant coming down the hallway and then there was a loud pounding on my door. When I opened it a crack, Angie, Jake's bodyguard, confronted me.

"What are you doing here?"

"I'm here to see Mr. Gottlieb," I answered, opening the door wide. "I flew all the way from New York to see him."

"You are not seeing him," he said bluntly.

Angie was 6'4", and weighed more than 350 pounds, and he was extremely muscular and fit. I was 5'4" and 120 pounds.

"Angie, you are not telling me what to do, and you are not scaring me one bit. I'm not leaving until I see him," I answered. I was used to seeing Angie be subservient to Jake and thought I could bend him to my will too.

Well, I was wrong.

"I'll give you a choice," Angie replied. "You can leave in the trunk of my car, or you can leave on the next flight out of here. Either way, you are not seeing him."

I think Angie was afraid Jake would give me money or name me in his will. I decided it would be more comfortable to leave on an airplane, and never did see Jake alive again, though I attended his funeral in Chicago to pay my last respects—despite receiving a warning to stay away. Dave Goldstein, the pit boss from the Dunes, accompanied me.

The universe is an unbelievable place. We do not always know when we have a profound influence on someone else's life. Your care and concern for others, and your generous acts, can help someone make a 360-degree turn, though you may never even know it.

Jake recognized qualities in me before I knew I possessed them. His admiration gave me the confidence, stamina and moxie I needed to prevail over enormous challenges in the years after he passed through my life.

I look upon Jake as a blessing from God. In the end, I didn't need to see him as he lay dying because his impact lived on and endures. Jake's influence on me is one of the reasons I continue to give and help others. He showed me giving has the power to affect hundreds of lives.

Jake changed my life for the better, though I only knew him for a few years. To this day, before I have my first sip of wine in the evening, I raise my glass and offer a toast of gratitude: "Here's to you, Jake."

DREAM BIG, ADD MOXIE

Jake sent Darlene a new Cadillac for many years, starting in 1961. The old Caddy was taken away when the new one was delivered—but not before Darlene struck this pose!

CLOCKWISE FROM ABOVE
Darlene at her newly constructed Kingston KFC, 1967; Darlene & Wally, late 1990s; Darlene speaking at one of the AKFCF conventions; and Darlene, the Colonel and husband Jan Headlee at KFC convention in late 1960s.

FACING PAGE
Top – Darlene's KFC, Kingston NY; bottom – Peter and Bevy circa 1969.

PART THREE

The KFC Years
Working Fearlessly

Top – 1st KFC store construction in 1967.
Bottom – One of Darlene's KFC stores.

CHAPTER 12

Start Small, Add Moxie and Stay the Course

Some life decisions start from following your gut. If you trust your instincts, add solid research, and gather input from those with experience, you can cook up a proven recipe for success.

In 1966, my husband, Jan Headlee, and I were driving from our home in Saugerties to Columbus, Ohio to visit our parents. It was a 12-hour drive, and I couldn't wait to get to the Kentucky Fried Chicken in Columbus! There weren't any KFCs—or any other franchises like McDonald's or Dunkin' Donuts—where we lived in Upstate New York.

"Jan, wouldn't it be great to have a fast-food restaurant in Kingston?" I said. "You know how much I love KFC. I'm going to investigate what it would take to bring a KFC to Kingston."

When we stopped to get gas, I made a call from a phone booth. That's the way I've always been—if I get an idea, I can't wait to put things in motion right away. I put a coin in the slot, dialed 0, asked the operator to connect me with the Kentucky Fried Chicken office in Ohio and fortuitously got connected to Dave Thomas' office. I set up a meeting with him for the very next day.

Dave Thomas was hired by KFC founder Colonel Harland Sanders to revive four failing KFC stores in Columbus. He made them profitable again, and by 1968, he sold them back to the corporation for more than $1.5 million. In 1969, after a brief stint as part of an investor group that founded Arthur Treacher's Fish & Chips, Dave founded the first Wendy's on East Broad Street in Columbus.

When I met with Dave, he was still re-energizing the Columbus KFC franchises. His motto was KISS—Keep It Simple Stupid—and that's just the way he talked to me about running a franchise.

"I'm just as common as an old shoe, honey. If I can do this, anyone can do this. It's the best business in the world. You've got to get involved with it."

He told me, "It's so simple, honey. You get all these chickens delivered to your back door and you cook 'em up. If you keep track of every piece you cook, every piece you sell, every piece you throw away because it falls on the floor, every piece your employees eat—if you keep track of every piece, you'll make money."

I was a pretty, 27-year-old woman and everybody called me "Honey."

What Dave said sounded simple to me. I thought, "Hell, I've been counting passengers for seven years as a flight attendant. I can count chickens. At least they stand still."

My conversation with Dave motivated me. When Jan and I returned to New York, I drove to Pittsfield, Massachusetts to meet a couple who owned a KFC. I quizzed them about the ins and outs of running a KFC and decided to go into the franchise business.

I flew to the national KFC offices in Nashville. I made a hit with all the men—and all the people working in positions of power were men, of course. I met with the vice president of KFC franchises and said I wanted to buy one.

"One? Oh honey, you don't want one—you want five!"

"I do?"

"Yes, you do," he said. "These are going so fast you've got to get more while you still can."

So I applied to buy franchises in Upstate New York in Kingston, Poughkeepsie, Newburgh and Middletown, and one in Danbury, Connecticut. I thought, "OK, that's easy. I got them all."

But it wasn't quite that simple.

I had started saving before I was born—my father's boss, Lou Dorman, gave my dad seven dollars to celebrate my birth and set up my first savings account—and every time I got a little extra money, I put it in the bank. I saved every penny I could from childhood on. A man who spoke to our flight attendant training class told us, "You're used to living on what you make today. Every time you get a raise, put it into your savings account," and that's what I did. When Jake and I went to the racetrack at Aqueduct, he'd bet for me using his own money and give me his winnings. I'd take that $20 or $50 and put it in my account.

By the time I married Jan and left TWA in 1965, I had saved $20,000 and had some capital invested in stocks too. The books I read on diversification advised people to never keep their money in just one place, because it might not succeed, so I purchased shares of five Blue Chip stocks—Xerox, AT&T, IBM and others. I had $2,000 here, $5,000 there, but was by no stretch well heeled.

After I sent my financial statement to KFC, I got a call from Maureen McGuire, who asked me if I had applied for five franchises. When I replied yes, she said, "Well, you can't have them. You have to have $20,000 in liquid cash per franchise."

Now I was dealing with a woman—not with all the men who were impressed by me.

"How much does my financial statement say I have?" I asked, though I knew the answer. I had filled out the paperwork myself.

"That's only enough for one," said McGuire.

"Oh my God, my accountant made a terrible mistake!" I said. "You send that financial statement right back to me. I've got to see where he made this mistake and correct it."

When I received the returned application, I added zeros to all the stock I had and returned it to her. In those days, you could call a bank and get a bank balance over the phone. But if you had stock, they wanted proof, and I told Maureen I would not send it through the mail.

"It might get lost," I said, thinking, *Why not? I'll try it and if they catch me, I'll throw out Dave Thomas' name and tell them he said I needed five stores.*

When I told my accountant in Saugerties I would be running five KFC franchises, he said, "That's the stupidest idea I've ever heard. More people are going into the franchise business and they're broke now. You'll never succeed."

I replied, "Well, I'm gonna try."

I figured when I made money on the first store, I would invest it in the second, so I bought the store in Kingston and leased the others. If I had it to do over again, I would have leased them all to have more cash on hand.

Very few women owned fast food franchises in 1967 when I started my first Kentucky Fried Chicken franchise in Kingston—and those who did had a man's signature on the paperwork. Before I could get my restaurant, I had to sign 51 percent of my ownership over to my husband. If a woman wanted to own a business of any kind—even if she had enough for a down payment, which was half of what I wanted to borrow—it just wasn't possible.

When I asked the bank president why I had to have my husband co-sign the loan application, he said, "Because you're a woman. You could get pregnant and not pay off the loan."

The Women's Business Ownership Act of 1988 (also known as HR 5050) was finally signed 21 years later, and it opened doors for women entrepreneurs. But until then, women were not permitted to borrow money or have a credit card without a male relative or male business partner as co-signer. I used my $20,000 savings and the $40,000 I borrowed from Jake for the down payment to purchase the land for my first store, but I needed to secure a business loan to construct my new KFC building and buy equipment. I had to give Jan control to get my bank loan. I thought, "That's not so bad. He's my husband. He can have control."

Once the first store was operational, I calculated I'd need 10 months to save enough money to begin building each of my other four stores. It took about five years before all of them were up and running. For my stores outside of Kingston, I leased the land instead of purchasing it to save some money, and then built the buildings.

After I started building my first KFC franchise in Kingston,

I went to stay with the couple in Pittsfield, Massachusetts, and they taught me a lot about how to run the business. I learned how to make the salads, but more than that, they showed me how they kept their sales books, sales lists, how to calculate taxes, and how to keep track of inventory and records. I went into it all a little blindly and didn't really consider whether I was capable of running a franchise.

In the spring of 1967 shortly after I opened my Kingston store, I got a visit from a young New York Life Insurance agent, Paul DeLisio. He had just finished college and had left the service, was married and had two small children. He sold me a health insurance and employee benefits package. He got to know some of my employees, and we had a few meetings in my office at the store.

I attended a weeklong KFC school to learn how to cook the chicken in a 20-quart pressure cooker, just like Colonel Sanders did it. When the chicken was done cooking, you had to carry it in the boiling hot shortening across a greasy floor—which was hard, especially for a small woman like me—over to a dump table where the shortening drained off into a holding tank. The chicken was racked immediately, bone side down, to drain for 15 minutes before serving. The Colonel never let the chicken stay in the shortening and never served it right out of the pressure cooker, which is how it remained so crispy and delicious. KFC got rid of the dump table about 40 years ago, but that's the way we did it in the beginning. We learned everything from how to do all the ordering to working behind the counter, all of which I did when I first started.

When you're running a business—any business—you have to watch the costs very carefully. I've always taken note of the prices of everything. It's innate in me, starting when I was a little girl shopping for my mother. I learned how to live on a budget while buying groceries for our meals.

When I first opened my KFC business, I did everything myself. I'd get to the store at 8:00 a.m. and work until 10:00 p.m., opening and closing every day. I was there all the time. I used to carry a little 25-caliber gun—I still have it—so I'd have some protection in case I was robbed, or if somebody came into the store or followed me when I was making the bank deposit, which was only about $700 or $800.

I began to attend the Northeast Regional KFC Franchise meetings and learned more about keeping track of inventory from my fellow franchisees. I remembered, and passed along, what Dave Thomas had told me: "Don't just look at the chicken." We all counted the chicken every night, but Dave said, "Keep track of your paper goods too. If you're using an awful lot of boxes—more than you're selling on your cash register—there's something wrong there."

The great thing about the KFC franchisees was we picked up a lot of knowledge from sharing with each other. Thanks to the business model established by Colonel Sanders, who started the business as a family-run operation, we stuck together like a family. I attribute a lot of our success as franchisees to his concept of banding together as a business family.

In the 1960s and '70s, the introduction of fast food and the development of the interstate highway system in the United States helped create a wide-open business environment for franchising. Though KFC franchisees had more independence than those operating in other franchises, KFC required more startup money and its approval process was more difficult. McDonald's, for example, bought the land and built buildings and franchisees had to lease from them—and were also required to live within a certain radius from the business—essentially controlling their franchisees completely.

KFC franchisees figured out together, by trial and error, how to be successful but these days, fewer people own one, two or five franchises. Now, big owners often buy multiple franchises—some own hundreds of stores—and the feeling of camaraderie that prevailed in earlier days has largely disappeared.

By leaning on each other, and sharing our knowledge, successes and challenges, we established KFC franchise business practices that were recognized as a model among franchisees in the United States. And I quickly stepped into a leadership role in an industry that continues to be a lucrative way to make a living.

Darlene and Jan at her newly constructed Kingston KFC, 1967.

CHAPTER 13

Build Your Own Family

*Whether formed with, or without, a great deal of forethought—
and whether created in blood, marriage or as an instinctual choice—
being part of a family can be one of life's most enduring commitments
and comforts. Yet families only become strong and healthy with
regular infusions of honesty, love, planning, humor and
an occasional dose of fierce protectiveness.*

When I hired the first group of people to work at my Kingston Kentucky Fried Chicken store, a very determined young man carrying a trumpet case applied for a job.

"I'm only fifteen years old," he told me, "but I can give you a man's day of work."

How could I not hire him?

I gave Peter Stoll a job. I later learned his father had died six years earlier. His mother, Nancy, cleaned houses and took care of a funeral home to support Peter and his little sister, Bevy. An older brother, Vincent, was married and lived in a trailer not far from them.

I took Peter under my wing, helped him with his English, and talked with him. He was a happy-go-lucky, yet sometimes serious, kid.

"What did you learn at school today?" I'd ask when he came into work. "Let me hear what you're playing on your trumpet."

One day, he was learning "The Lonely Bull," a tune made famous by Herb Alpert and the Tijuana Brass. I had him go inside the walk-in cooler to play it for us so it wouldn't bother customers, and he sounded pretty good.

He and I became close so when he looked dejected one day, I asked, "What's wrong Peter? You're so happy all the time."

"My mom's in the hospital. She had to have a breast removed. She has cancer."

"Well, do you want to go see her?"

"I'm scared. I can't go."

"I'll go with you," I said, and took him to visit Nancy at the hospital.

I first met Bevy and her mother a couple of weeks later when Nancy got out of the hospital and invited me to visit her. We were seated in her living room, talking, when I noticed a blonde, blue-eyed girl hiding behind Nancy's chair. She was looking at me, but Nancy never introduced her daughter. Bevy just kept watching me from behind the chair. She was born in 1960 and was eight years old.

"As you know, Darlene, I have cancer," Nancy said.

"Yes."

"And, Peter really loves and respects you."

"Thank you."

"If anything happens to me, would you take Peter?"

"Of course," I said, "but what's going to happen to Bevy?"

"She'll have to go to Maine to live with an elderly aunt of mine," she replied nonchalantly.

"Oh no, she'll be with Peter and me," I said.

I wasn't hesitant—it never entered my mind to not take Bevy in—and I never discussed my decision first with my husband, Jan. This was 1968 and I was 32. I had just started my first Kentucky Fried Chicken store in Kingston the year before and was busy building four more stores. But nothing would stop me.

Nancy lived for another year and a half, and I wanted Bevy to be with her mother as much as possible during that time, so I didn't intrude. I did invite the Stolls to my house for Thanksgiving and Christmas dinners and other family occasions so we could get to know each other a little better.

When Nancy became really sick and returned to the hospital, Peter asked if he could bring Bevy to stay with me.

"Of course. Bring her."

That night, I heard pounding on my front door and when I looked out, there was a large, very imposing, New York State Trooper standing there.

"Are you harboring one Beverly Stoll in this house?"

"I'm not harboring her. She's staying with me."

"We've got a report she was kidnapped."

"If you want to speak with her, step inside please and you can talk with her. She's consenting to be here. She's happy to be here."

The officer spoke with Bevy and was evidently satisfied because he left. But that was scary.

On her deathbed, Nancy realized there were some family issues with how her estate would be split and who would care for Bevy and Peter. She immediately called her attorney to make all the arrangements for her children and named me legal guardian.

That's how I got Bevy without a court battle: It was a mother's desire. Little Bevy stayed with me until her mother died, and then came to live with me when she was 10, a year-and-a-half after her mother had gotten sick.

Peter and Bevy circa 1969.

Peter lived with me for a couple of years, then wanted to spread his wings. I got him an apartment in a tiny little house across the street from us and he loved it. He earned his associate degree from Ulster County Community College, then got an accounting degree from Marist College. When he married his high school sweetheart, we all attended the wedding before they moved to Colorado. Peter worked as an auditor and he and his wife had three children—a daughter and a set of twins (a boy and a girl). Like his father before him and his own young son, Peter succumbed to heart disease at an early age. He died in 2013 of a heart attack when he was only 60 years old.

Bevy and I got, and remain, extremely close. From the beginning, I always wanted her to have the best of what I could provide for her.

I took Bevy to school every day, first to the Chambers School, and then to The Kingston Academy. When the Academy closed, I investigated several private schools for her to continue her education, and found a wonderful finishing school, The Emma Willard Girls School in Troy, New York.

When Bevy was in the 10th grade, I enrolled her at Emma Willard, tuition free, because she had no money. Since I had never formally adopted her, she received monthly Social Security checks and I saved them for her for college. It hurt me a great deal to send Bevy away to this boarding school that was more than an hour away from where we lived in Saugerties.

I already knew my husband Jan was not a Joe Faithful kind of guy—he was running around and having an affair with a waitress at that time—and he had some other real problems too. His behavior towards Bevy worried me and I was instinctually concerned for her.

Bevy and I talked about it later, and she never said anything against Jan. By the time she graduated in 1977, Jan and I had split up and Bevy came back home to live with me.

Giving extends to how we give of ourselves, not just monetarily. At the time when Bevy first came into my life, I didn't stop to think, *what am I going to do with this kid? How will I afford to take care of her? I have so much else going on, how will I give her the love and attention she needs, especially when my life is already busy and complicated?*

I didn't think about any of that.

One little girl needed me, and I trusted everything would work out OK. Making a family with Bevy was one of the best, most intuitive, choices I ever made, and our life together is one of my greatest joys. She is an extraordinary person. Today we're not only the best of buddies, we love each other deeply. It's just a God-given miracle this happened to us.

Darlene and Bevy circa 2000s.

DREAM BIG, ADD MOXIE

Bevy Hung's Perspective: Part 1

My mom, Nancy Stoll, was a single mom so I had to be taken care of after school while she worked. I went to Virginia's day care down the street from our house. When my mom was sick and dying from cancer, I thought I'd go live with Virginia because she already took care of me. But family issues arose with our relatives, and Darlene came into our lives. I don't really remember that part, but I asked my mom questions about where I would go to live after she passed away.

"You're going to live with Darlene, and you'll be treated like a princess for the rest of your life," my mom said.

She told me just like that. I trusted my mother and didn't question it, even though everything seemed up in the air.

Before my mom died, I went to kiss Darlene goodbye once after we were visiting—her cheeks were full and so soft, like a pillow—and she was so nice. She was dressed in a white outfit with gold buttons and had beautiful nails. I was in awe of her.

Looking back, I think, "Wow, what a bold move for my mother to select Darlene, and for Darlene to take on the responsibility." They didn't know each other well, didn't have a prior relationship. It was very odd, but also wonderful, like in *Lifetime* movies on TV.

When I went to live with Darlene and Jan in 1970, I was just 10 years old. I'd never had parents in a traditional way. "Look at my parents," I'd think. I was so proud. It helped me get over losing my mom and, since Darlene and Jan both had parents, now I had grandparents too.

Darlene took me to the hairdresser and let me pick out clothes I liked at the store. She was never into labels and all that—she had her own style, like Dolly Parton—and she tried to find the style I liked and would buy me beautiful clothes. On our first Christmas together, she got all my presents from

DARLENE L. PFEIFFER

Flah's Department Store, and everything was pink—the whole living room and all the presents!

Darlene took her mother (Louise) and me to New York City one Christmas and we stayed at the Plaza Hotel—it was really beautiful! She didn't want to pay for a bigger room so when she saw the maid's closet, which was where they kept the cots, she got one and set it up.

We saw the Rockettes at Radio City Music Hall and went to the Oak Room at the Plaza, where we saw David Frost. I was so excited. Louise was a character and said—in a really loud voice—"Oh yes, that's him, but he looks terrible!" We weren't that far away from him and I'm sure he heard her. I thought I'd die.

We had dinner at Mamma Leone's in the Theater District and everybody ate a little too much. Darlene's dog, JG, got sick during the night. She was by my side and when I went to pick her up, the whole bed collapsed. I was laughing and so was Louise because it was so funny. When Louise laughed, it sounded like passing gas, which made me laugh even more. Darlene was not as amused. The next day, the toilet in our room got stopped up so Darlene took us to the lobby to use the bathroom and Jackie O—Jacqueline Kennedy Onassis—was there!

On the way home, the windshield wipers on our old borrowed car didn't work properly and we were in a terrible ice storm. Darlene had wanted that trip to be so perfect, and we had so much fun and made many good memories, despite all of the mishaps.

Darlene and I have a lovely life together, with a lot of extra-curricular activities. My upbringing wasn't typical, but it was certainly magical. The things she did for her husband, Jan, she did for me—lovely dinners, notes in my lunchbox. I feel blessed and lucky.

CHAPTER 14

Mentor: Colonel Sanders
A Recipe for Giving

Being a mentor, and setting an inspiring example for others, is one of the most important roles you can play in life. By supporting the profound changes one person is trying to make, a mentor's positive influence has the potential to completely alter the course of the lives of countless others.

Colonel Sanders was a generous man who lived fearlessly. I loved him and considered him a mentor. He worked hard—and failed, usually through no fault of his own—at many different business ventures before he hit on his life-changing Kentucky Fried Chicken success.

He was born Harland David Sanders in 1890 in Henryville, Indiana, and he grew up poor, the eldest of three children. His father died when he was only five years old. Like me, when his widowed mother had to go get a job (my mother took a clerical job working for the state of Ohio; his worked at a tomato cannery), he assumed the responsibility of cooking for his mother and his siblings. Sanders worked many jobs as a teenager—farmhand, streetcar conductor, blacksmith's helper, steam engine stoke—and met his wife, Josephine King, at age 19, when he was a railroad laborer. They had three children—a son, Harland, Jr., who died young, and two daughters, Margaret and Mildred.

Over the next three decades, Sanders worked at a variety of projects and jobs. He owned and sold a successful ferry boat company that transported passengers across the Ohio River, then established another company which manufactured acetylene lamps. He worked as a tires salesman and in the 1930s, ran a service station and adjoining restaurant in Corbin, Kentucky, where he first attracted acclaim for tasty fried chicken dinners made from his secret recipe.

When he ran the service station, he always cooked for his family. But before he'd let his wife and two children sit down for a meal, he'd say, "Don't eat it yet. Let me see if the truckers want to eat it," and he'd first offer the meals he prepared to truckers passing through the small town.

"I've got some good vittles here. Come on in and have some!"

He sat the truckers down at the family kitchen table and as word spread, added a few more tables. To handle increasing demand, Sanders went out and got a new-fangled pressure cooker, which was developed around that time. Frying chicken was normally a messy, dirty job that took 30 to 35 minutes and made a greasy mess of the stovetop, but with the pressure cooker, he could serve more meals faster. It only took 12 minutes to fry chicken in the pressure cooker—a big change that meant easier cleanup, too. Sanders developed his method of cooking with a pressure cooker and experimented with his recipe by adding herbs and spices.

"Daughter! Come here and taste this," he'd say to Margaret.

After many tries, she finally said, "I think you've got it, Dad!"

He tacked a hand-written recipe on the door frame of the kitchen where he had perfected his secret recipe and expanded the restaurant to hold more tables and chairs. He also added a small motel to his tiny complex of service station, restaurant and lodging on the main highway from Kentucky to Florida, which became famous. The Sanders Court and Café even got a good review in *Adventures in Good Eating*, a popular guide to US restaurants published in 1939 by food critic Duncan Hines, later known for his own line of food products.

When the restaurant and motel burned down, Sanders rebuilt it as a 140-seat restaurant and motel, but World War II negatively impacted his plans as travel and tourism became luxuries. He took jobs in Seattle and Tennessee for a few years and divorced his wife in 1947, marrying his longtime mistress, Claudia Ledington-Price, two years later. By 1952, he was ready to concentrate on his delicious chicken recipe once again. That year, Colonel Sanders franchised his Kentucky Fried Chicken recipe for the first time to one of the largest restaurants in Utah. When the restaurant's sales more than tripled in the first year of selling his fried chicken, Sanders franchised the concept to several more restaurants.

Three years later, when Sanders turned 65 and the new Interstate Highway 75 bypassed his North Corbin, Kentucky, complex, his thriving restaurant went belly up so he closed it up and declared bankruptcy. Armed with his secret recipe, his trusty pressure cooker, a monthly Social Security check of $105, a car and his own tenacity, Sanders took to the road.

As a member of the National Restaurant Association, he drove around Indiana and Kentucky, determined to drum up business by showing other restauranteurs how to cook chicken his way. After his demonstration in the kitchen, he would take off his apron, put on his white suit, and go out and be "the Colonel" with the customers.

If the restaurant owners liked the chicken and wanted to offer it to their customers, Sanders negotiated the rights to use his seasoning, leased a pressure cooker to them, charged them four cents a head for each chicken (nine pieces) that they sold, and set up an agreement to supply them with his 11 herbs and spices. He sealed the deal with a handshake and never used a signed contract, but his method of doing business was brilliant: if the restauranteur didn't cook the chicken his way, Sanders would do what he called "pulling the pots," meaning he pulled his pressure cooker out of their kitchen.

He patented his method of pressure frying chicken in 1962 and the next year, trademarked the phrase "It's Finger Lickin' Good." From then on, he devoted his energies to building a vast network of restaurants to sell his fast food chicken with the unifying principle of creating a family of restauranteurs.

Sanders didn't have money to stay at motels while traveling around to offer demonstrations of how to cook his chicken, so when restaurant owners were kind enough to ask, "Where are you staying tonight?" he would reply, "I haven't made reservations yet."

"Come stay with us!" most of his customers said, giving

him a bed to sleep in rather than the back seat of his car. In this way, he built a family-style network of Kentucky Fried Chicken franchisees. Every time he brought a new franchisee onboard, Sanders visited them and kept in touch, creating a business model that felt more like family than any other franchise group.

Years later, when I led the National Association of KFC Franchisees and we encountered problems, I was fighting for my KFC family. I would not give up and we prevailed, time and again. My instincts were correct: A professor at Cornell University who was writing his doctoral dissertation on franchisee relationships told me KFC had the only franchisee network that was able to protect their rights despite corporate attempts to diminish them. He said this success was largely due to the way the Colonel established and nurtured our franchisees' sense of being part of a family, a model that remained strong until about 2010.

I admired the way Colonel Sanders picked himself up, brushed himself off, faced down poverty again and again and, through sheer determination and force of will, built one of the first fast food chains to go international. By 1964, there were more than 600 KFC locations. That year, he sold the remaining franchising rights (some others had previously been sold) to John Y. Brown, who would later become the governor of Kentucky, and venture capitalist/entrepreneur, Jack C. Massey. Sanders earned $2 million (more than $16 million in today's dollars), retained Canadian operations and took on the role of salaried KFC brand ambassador.

Colonel Sanders moved to Canada in 1965 to oversee his Canadian franchises, but he traveled 200,000 miles annually, filmed TV commercials, and received appearance fees, all while wearing his distinctive Southern gentleman's white coat, black string tie and white goatee, always playing the part of the Colonel to the hilt. He helped franchisees enormously by making public appearances at their restaurants.

I first met the Colonel at KFC conventions when I was a

new franchisee. Like everyone else, I stood in line to have my picture taken with him, and still treasure those photographs. He was a ladies' man who liked pretty girls and he always made everyone feel like they knew him. When he walked in the room, he made it easy and comfortable to start a conversation with him.

In 1977, after I got back four of my nine KFC restaurants in my divorce settlement, I was intent on making my businesses a success. I called Sanders' secretary, Shirley Topmiller, and said, "I know the Colonel often visits franchisees' stores. What do you think of the possibility of him coming to visit my Kingston restaurant?"

"Oh, I know he'll be thrilled," she said.

Sure enough, the Colonel came to Kingston later that year, and returned a couple of years later when I opened my Poughkeepsie restaurant on South Road. Both times, he stayed at my house, which he still preferred to staying at a hotel.

The first time he came, I picked him up at 8:00 a.m. at LaGuardia Airport. Everyone knew who he was. He always

Darlene, the Colonel and husband Jan Headlee at KFC convention in late 1960s.

wore his trademark white suit—linen in summer and wool in winter—with his string tie, and with his white goatee and hair and a beaming smile, he greeted everyone in his recognizable Southern accent. When he started out, he didn't have any money to spend on advertising, so he became the spokesperson for his new baby, the Kentucky Fried Chicken brand, and he was a brilliant marketer.

"Oh look! There's the Colonel!" Everyone came up to him for his autograph. I was afraid some kid with chocolate on their hands would hug him and ruin his white suit—the only one he brought with him—as I tripped alongside him, trying to keep him moving through the mob scene.

"Yes," I said, hooking my arm through his, "and he's my Colonel for two days." That was such a proud moment for me.

When we got to Kingston, I took him to lunch at Judy's Restaurant, and then to my KFC store. We arrived at 2:00 p.m. and people were lined up all around the store, waiting to meet him. He sat at a table for hours, signing autographs, talking with people and having his picture taken with customers. We used a Polaroid camera and gave each person their photo with him to take home—some people still display theirs proudly on their wall.

After a few hours, I suggested we wrap things up and go to my house, where I had cooked a nice dinner for him. I had found out from Shirley what he liked, and had prepared flounder, limburger cheese and other favorite dishes.

But he cocked his head to the side and said, "I can still hear the piano player playing," referring to the cash register ringing. He sat there until 6:00 p.m. when I had to drag him out. After we finished our meal at my house, I was worn out. I had gotten up early to drive to the airport and suggested we go to bed. But he wanted to go back to my store and asked, "What time does your store close down?"

"Nine o'clock," I told him.

"We're going back to Kentucky Fried Chicken. I'm going to teach you how to make gravy!"

And just like that, he got up from the dinner table, and bolted down the stairs. I was running after him, trying to keep up. He was tireless, even at 87 years old. That night, he showed me and my staff how to make his gravy, which was his special passion.

The next morning, I hosted an 8:00 a.m. breakfast for him at the Governor Clinton Hotel. I couldn't afford to have a big event with a dinner for the press, but I wanted him to be interviewed by the local media. He spoke about his life—how he came into this world very poor, his restaurant in Corbin, Kentucky, and how he built his hugely successful empire—and ended with his philosophy on giving: "I entered this world with nothing and I'm going to give it all away!"

He sat next to me for the breakfast, which was Eggs Benedict, and he thought it was fancy.

"Honey, how much did you have to pay for this?" he asked me. "This looks expensive."

I explained it wasn't. "It's just an English muffin cut in half, and piled up with Canadian bacon, poached eggs, Hollandaise sauce and a sprinkle of herbs."

When the Colonel returned two years later for the opening of my new restaurant in Poughkeepsie, he did the same thing—photos with customers, an evening meal with me, a media event—and he insisted on teaching everyone who worked at my KFC how to make the gravy. I told him we were making it according to how the company told us to do it, but he said it wasn't right.

"I wouldn't feed that gravy to my prize hog," he boomed. He showed us how to mix the ingredients, adding water and cracklins until it was perfect. In the midst of our lesson, he excused himself to go to the bathroom and when he returned, the cooks were standing there, waiting, all decked out in their uniforms with chefs' hats on, but no one was attending the gravy. It was starting to boil over.

"What's going on here? Why didn't somebody take care of this gravy? Doesn't anybody work here?!" he bellowed in a harsh tone, surveying the kitchen. One young man in particular had a look of pure terror on his face. No one wanted to disappoint the Colonel.

"I knew you Yankees were dumb," he yelled, reverting back to his Southern roots, "but I didn't know you were this dumb!"

All I could think was, *I've gotta get him out of here,* so I said, "We've got to leave, Colonel. We've got a plane to catch."

His gravy, method of pressure frying and special recipe of 11 herbs and spices, along with his Southern hospitality and image, were his claim to fame, and he was fierce about making sure everything was prepared and presented in the proper way. He had very high standards and made sure we followed them: The Colonel never let his franchisees down, but he expected the best from everyone. Colonel Sanders was a fighter who made a lasting impression on everyone who met him and helped create a Kentucky Fried Chicken family.

Before he died in Louisville, Kentucky at the age of 90, he established a registered Canadian charity and funded a hospital wing for women and children, made sizable donations to several children's hospitals, and contributed to numerous other charities. As the Colonel told me, "I came into this life poor, and I'm going to leave the same way. I'm going to give it all away before I die."

He did put money into a trust for his daughters, but it wasn't lavish. When his daughter Margaret got married for the fourth time, the Colonel gave her all the franchises in the state of Florida for a wedding present. She maintained ownership, and then gave them to her sons and daughters. Margaret was always more interested in making art than in chicken. She didn't make a lot of money from her franchises, but she definitely lived comfortably.

"Who cares what you have when they lower you into the grave? What's important is what you do while you're here on earth," the Colonel often said.

His philosophy and commitment to help others is one reason why I am a passionate advocate for scholarship programs, both at the KFC and at SUNY Ulster, and why I give to other organizations that help and inspire people. He showed me and so many others how much influence one person can have. We were friends until he died and his family invited me to his funeral.

Prior to creating the Kentucky Fried Chicken empire, Sanders ran a small restaurant. Every Thanksgiving and Christmas, he and his wife closed the place to the public and gave their employees the day off to be with their loved ones. Then the Sanderses rented an old school bus and picked up 25 children from an orphanage that was "down the road a piece." They brought the children to their restaurant to serve them a dinner they had cooked especially for them to make sure they had a delicious and festive meal.

When the Colonel established his Kentucky Fried Chicken restaurants, he closed all of them on those two holidays and he and his wife continued their annual tradition. Few people know why KFCs are always closed on Thanksgiving and Christmas, but I've never forgotten his kindness—not only to his employees but to the children who lived at the orphanage.

Throughout his life Colonel Sanders led by example, and although he crafted a distinctive public persona, he didn't brag about what he did for other people. I share his belief that one of the best things you can do in life is to give of yourself to help others. When you give, your influence and inspiration continue long after you are gone from this physical plane because, as the Colonel believed and as I do too, giving is eternal.

CHAPTER 15

Keep Moving Forward

You cannot always predict where your actions will lead you. If you start your journey with conviction and feed that feeling with every step you take, you'll be in a much stronger position than where you began. Keep climbing, slow and steady, and you can prevail over any obstacle. Any success in life starts with just one thing—believing in the power of YOU.

I started dating Jan Headlee when I was about 18 years old and we were both still living in Columbus, Ohio. He was 6'2" tall, handsome and beautifully built. At that time, he was always looking in the mirror and I would say to him, "Jan, it's more important to develop the beauty within than what you carry outwardly. Outward beauty can be taken away from you at any time."

He called me Grandma Moses of the Mountain because I was so serious, but I meant it. Six months later, his car was hit by a train and he ended up with a scar that ran across his face. He was just as handsome, but what I said was prophetic: Your looks can be wiped away in seconds, but you'll always have what's within. I thought he was a really good guy, but there was something within him he couldn't control. Possibly he got that from his grandfather, because his grandmother stayed with me for a while, and told me her husband was just like Jan—a vain woman chaser.

I started my first KFC restaurant in 1967. Remember, since married women in those days could not obtain bank loans without the signature of their husband, I had given my husband 51 percent ownership to get the loan to build it. Jan had his own business as a casket salesman, yet he retained controlling interest of my business while I built and ran my first three stores. When he saw they were a success, he decided I needed his help: Together we built two more stores, but he wasn't much involved on a daily basis.

By the time I had established all five KFC stores, Jan decided he wanted complete control of my business. He stepped in, used the equity from my first five stores to build four more stores of his own without putting my name on any of them, and told me he wanted me out of the KFC business. He started telling me I was crazy and too demanding of him.

Our marriage was not working, so I went to a marriage counselor to try to figure out how I could save it. I thought I should start another business, but I realized from my therapy sessions that Jan considered me a threat. When my marriage counselor suggested I get out of the business, I decided to go back to finish my college degree at SUNY New Paltz. I had sent Bevy to boarding school at Emma Willard in the fall of the previous year. I separated from Jan early in 1975 and devoted myself to my studies. Initially, our separation was friendly, but once lawyers got involved, it turned ugly and expensive.

I earned my bachelor's degree in political science and graduated summa cum laude in 1976, which had the unintended effect of making me an even bigger threat to Jan's ego. My professors all loved me as I was an older student, in my 30s, and I worked very hard, but I finally realized there was no way I could win in my marriage.

I had tried everything, but fighting Jan to get my stores from him turned into a big legal battle. We both had New York attorneys representing us, and at one meeting his attorney said, "Jan will give you XYZ a year and you won't have to be in the business any longer. Of course, you won't be able to drive a Cadillac anymore; maybe you'll have to drive a Pontiac."

I said, "You tell Jan I've been driving a Cadillac since I was 23 years old and I'm not changing for anyone—not him, not anyone." I knew he wouldn't have paid me and would have cheated me out of the alimony.

One night, I went to his office—which was newly redecorated with an elaborate bar—and took all his financial records to my accountant's office and copied them. I returned them without leaving a trace and kept them as evidence, in case I needed them.

I learned Jan had taken a million-dollar life insurance

policy out on me and thought, *I'd better be careful with this man.* I wrote a letter to the local district attorney and told him my husband and I had separated, and I had recently discovered he had taken a sizable insurance policy out on my life. I stated, "Look to him as the first person who would be highly suspect in the case of my demise." I gave a copy of the letter to Jan with a dramatic note saying, "You'd better hope I don't get hit by a car or anything else happens to me, accidental or otherwise."

My divorce from Jan was decreed in January 1977, before equitable distribution laws were enacted in New York State. I got our main house on Pearl Street in Kingston and Jan got the house in Saugerties where my mother lived, so I moved her into another home.

Together Jan and I owned nine KFC stores: I got back three of them—one in Kingston and two in Poughkeepsie. Between lawyers' fees for our acrimonious divorce, and debts to creditors and the bank because Jan had skimmed money off the restaurants and wasn't paying the bills, I had to claw my way out of $140,000 of debt [comparable to $640,000 in 2021]. I ran my three stores by myself from 1977 until I retired from the franchise business in 2019.

My daughter, Bevy, graduated from high school in the spring of 1977, and wanted to go to college but we hit a brick wall: I didn't have enough money to send her to college and because Jan and I had split up, he controlled all the money and refused to help. Bevy began working at my Kingston KFC, and fell in love with Walt, the store manager, who was closer to my age than hers. She had lost her dad when she was only two years old, and Walt was a nice guy, a father figure to her.

When Jan and I were still married and he was busy trying to take over my KFC stores, he allowed a lot of inappropriate relationships among employees. Employees were dating each other and having affairs, so when I met with the managers who stayed on with me after I got my stores back in the divorce settlement, I told them things had changed. There would be no fraternization among managers, customer service managers and assistant managers, and there would be no dating among their employees. If there were, I told them, they would have to quit or they would be fired.

So, when I found out Bevy was dating Walt—and they were sneaking around about it—I called them into my office.

"I know the two of you are seeing each other. I'm going to give you three choices," I said, reiterating the rules I had laid down. "Walt, you can quit as manager. Bevy, you can leave home. I can't have you living with me if you're dating a manager. Or the two of you can break up. Those are your choices."

Bevy moved out. I felt terrible. I loved her and felt bad because I had been so strict about enforcing my business principles. But I had three stores to run and was so opposed to how Jan had conducted business, and how awful he had been as an owner, I had to take a stand. Even though I loved her, as owner I couldn't have my own daughter breaking the rules and dating a manager.

Walt and Bevy got married, and she got a job at an insurance company. When her boss relocated the company to Florida, they moved down there and I got Walt a job at a KFC near their new home. They had a happy life together for 25 years until he passed away. Through it all, Bevy and I created a relationship that's strong and close. She calls me when she's going to work and when she gets home and whenever I go to Florida, we always have a great time when we're together.

Being straightforward with people is an asset, both in personal life and in business, because people like to know what to expect from you. It's not always easy to be direct and take a stand but learning to be assertive is essential. It's a leadership muscle that develops with practice, and it's especially effective when used for the right purposes. In business, taking a stand can build or strengthen a positive business culture. In your personal interactions, standing up for your beliefs reinforces the value of maintaining principles. Firmness is not the same as meanness, and it's important to know the difference.

DARLENE L. PFEIFFER

During those years, I basically kept my head down and worked hard every day to keep my businesses running smoothly and dig my way out of the debt my divorce left in its wake. I learned a lot in those years and got a better grip on what it takes to run a strong and successful franchise business.

Bevy Hung's Perspective: Part 2

The hard part for Mom—though she probably wouldn't say it—was she really did love Jan. When Darlene was a homemaker, she was the perfect wife. She spent more time at home because Jan wanted to be in charge of the businesses. When he came home, she was beautifully dressed in a gown and had a drink ready for him as he came through the door. Back then, wives were supposed to make a happy home and make their husbands comfortable. Magazines and books advised women to clean away clutter, take one last trip through the house to tidy up, and prepare themselves. *Take 15 minutes to refresh your makeup and put on a nice outfit. Make him a drink, ask him about his day and listen to him.* That's how it was. Comparing that to how she is today is amazing.

During the '60s and '70s, my mother evolved in her own quiet way. She finished her college degree at SUNY New Paltz and developed the part of herself that wanted more out of life. When they divorced and she got her KFC stores back—not her fair share, but she got what she got—the years with Jan helped set her trajectory from then on. I don't think she was conscious of this, but after Jan, she never let a man have that much control over her again. The walls went up, and I don't blame her: It helped her move along faster than other women did back in the day.

Our initial life together was pretty short-lived—I came to live with her when I was 10, was with her and Jan for a few years, and then went to Emma Willard School at age 15. That's a lot of changes for a person to go through and I didn't have the capacity to understand it all, but it did teach me independence. She always encouraged me to persist in getting an education. Going away to boarding school was a lot for a young girl to handle, especially because many of the girls were from very wealthy families and I was a bit out of my league. She taught me, as a woman, to take care of myself. During that time, she went on her career path and I went on my own path.

When she called Walt and me into her office at KFC to confront us about our relationship, that was pretty devastating. I felt not supported, of course, but I get it today as I look back on it. I knew I had to find my own way. Those were growing times. We didn't have a lot of interaction for a while.

She wasn't the type of person to identify herself as a feminist, but I think it's good for young women today to see how women evolved. They might not carry a flag to break down barriers—that's not everybody's personality—and she didn't have a mentor to show her the way. She just lived it. It wasn't her cause.

Back then, I remember seeing the history of the women's movement and women taking off their bras and protesting, but that wasn't her style. She always dressed perfectly. She got her nails done before others were doing it and carried her little dog JG in a Louis Vuitton bag long before anybody traveled with pets in carriers. She was very progressive in everything and she lived what feminists were espousing, certainly trailblazed the way forward with her own experiences. It was a big leap from flight attendant to businessperson—and selling chicken of all things—and it's kind of crazy in a good way. She took risks to pursue an unusual course and it worked out for her. She would have been bored if she'd done normal things: life gives you what you need.

DARLENE L. PFEIFFER

When I started my Kentucky Fried Chicken franchises in 1967, franchisees operating around the United States did not have an official way to communicate with or learn from each other. We were also unable to advocate for ourselves as a unified group operating within the structure of the Kentucky Fried Chicken Corporation (KFCC). This meant that although early franchisees helped each other as best we could, we had to learn to be successful without national support from the KFC network.

However, in the 1970s, the Association of KFC Franchisees (AKFCF) formed, and the first regional group emerged in the Southeast. When I attended the initial meeting of the Northeast region in 1977, the Southeast regional group had been active for five years, was relatively well established, and knew what they were doing.

Our Northeast regional Association of KFC Franchisees began holding two meetings each year, one at The Concord Hotel in the Catskills and one in Boston. We all ate together and got to know each other while discussing our business concerns. When we compared the costs of driving to Boston against $98 airline tickets, we decided to hold our springtime meeting in Florida. Those were formative years, both for our Northeast regional AKFCF and for me, as I gradually stepped into a leadership role, starting with our regional group.

As I got increasingly involved in the franchisees' nationwide systems and in helping all of us to communicate with each other to protect our business interests, corporate entities bought and sold Kentucky Fried Chicken. Networking was vital for individual franchisees in far-flung locations all across America who, like me, operated in somewhat of a vacuum. I realized the organization of the AKFCF was brilliant.

The AKFCF is an international federation of 11 different regional associations with its own board of directors. Six regional U.S. associations—in the Northeast, Southeast, Southwest, Great Lakes, Upper Midwest and in Southern California—created a direct pipeline of communication between the franchisees and the national organization. Even more importantly, these regional associations offered a unifying framework for franchisees to address issues of vital concern to their bottom lines.

The AKFCF worked with two U.S. committees: the National Franchisee Advisory Committee (NFAC) and the National Advertising Cooperative, Inc. (NAC). The latter was a separate non-profit corporation based in Delaware which had its own lawyers. I served in leadership positions on all three of them—the AKFCF, the NFAC and the NAC—during my 52 years with KFC.

In 1983, I took my initial step toward having an impact at the national level when the Northeast Region asked me to serve on the National Franchisee Advisory Committee (NFAC). Each region could also send one person to serve on the national board of directors of the AKFCF, which turned out to our advantage as I achieved greater levels of influence.

I became the first woman elected to serve on the national AKFCF. I worked my way up from second vice president to be the first woman voted the AKFCF president in 1988 and, when I returned to the office in 1995, I was the first person elected to serve twice as its president.

Darlene kissing the Colonel at KFC convention circa 1970; and Darlene speaking at one of the AKFCF conventions.

The franchisees were a stabilizing force because between 1964 and 2016, there were 20 different KFC presidents and several corporate owners. In 1964, Colonel Sanders sold KFC to John Y. Brown and Jack Massey, who got the company off the ground and grew it. KFC stock was a go-go mutual fund in those days, and investors focused on high-risk securities to obtain above average returns: KFC stock often split two for one and three for one in those days. This aggressive investing approach paid off and established KFC as a coveted growth stock. Brown and Massey then sold KFC to Heublein, an importer of liquor, and then to RJ Reynolds, the tobacco company. RJ Reynolds sold KFC to PepsiCo in 1986, and PepsiCo eventually split the company and KFC became a part of Tricon.

Heublein, RJ Reynolds and PepsiCo viewed KFC as a cash cow and didn't put money back into it. By contrast, McDonald's Corporation and its restaurants, whose average sales volume at that time was similar to KFC's, took a different approach. McDonald's concentrated on hamburgers, re-invested profits into the company, developed the brand and its marketing, along with its lines of new products, and enhanced the stores. McDonald's also tripled their advertising budget and installed drive-thru windows, an idea they took from Dave Thomas. Even though I didn't agree with all their franchising practices, McDonald's and other franchise companies did that part right.

As successive changes occurred in both corporate ownership and KFC's internal presidential tenures, franchisees had to be strong and form alliances to protect our rights. As president of the National Association of KFC Franchisees, I united a group of KFC franchisees that would stick with me. We had to be vigilant because the company would pull shenanigans, and we faced our biggest challenges during the decade when PepsiCo assumed ownership.

For me, it was a long journey from my decision to buy a KFC franchise to becoming the leader who faced off against the corporate giant, PepsiCo.

CHAPTER 16

Love and Local Service

Giving—whether it's your time, hard-won wisdom, compassion or financial support—extends your impact beyond the calendar of the years you spend on earth. Working on common goals with like-minded people makes all the difference.

I met Wally Pfeiffer in 1976 after I separated from Jan. He was president of the boards of directors of the YMCA and of the Wiltwyck Country Club, both in Kingston, New York, which is where we met each other socially. I heard him speak at a local Chamber of Commerce event, and he invited me to join the YMCA board during our conversation afterward.

Wally was separated from his wife—she had gone to Minneapolis to live—and we began dating. He had one child, Nick, who was in his 20s, and I was surprised to find he readily accepted me. Nick and I loved each other from the start and have been close ever since we met. Nick is a flight attendant and Wally had served as a meteorologist for Northwest Airlines in Alaska many years before, so we three had the airlines in our blood.

I didn't tell Wally I was divorced until several months after the papers were signed. I had no intention of getting married again, but Wally was persistent, and I finally accepted his proposal. We got married on December 24, 1977, in a beautiful wedding at my home.

Wally was a great man—he was the wind beneath my wings for 25 years. He was always there, in the background, doing whatever he could to make my life better. When I was secretary/treasurer of the AFKFC, he was an invaluable help to me, especially before computers became prevalent. Wally typed out our newsletters on a typewriter and took them to the printer, and then we assembled everything and prepared the mailings at our kitchen table.

The YMCA board was the first local board I served on,

and I held the office of president—and was the first woman president of the board—for two years at the beginning of the 1980s. The man who was executive director did a wonderful job but was used to being in total control and wasn't enthralled about having a woman as president of the board—especially when I questioned his unilateral decision to take Fridays off.

"I've noticed you take every Friday off," I said, during a meeting with him at my office.

"I work very hard when I am there," he countered.

"Well, so do most of your staff," I replied. "When they see you taking Fridays off, they will start to feel they are entitled to take Fridays off too. When you are in charge," I added, "you must set an example for your staff. You can take Fridays off, but I'm going to count those hours against your accrued vacation time. It's your choice."

He didn't like that. He was used to doing what he wanted.

I called him at his office every Friday afternoon at 4:00 p.m. I always had a good reason to call him—I wasn't trying to be mean, and I didn't just call to check up on him.

Every well-run organization requires vigilance, including overseeing scheduling.

I also served on the Kiwanis board and as their president for a couple of years and was briefly involved with the Ulster County Chamber of Commerce.

Today I serve on the boards of the SUNY Ulster Foundation and the Community Foundations of the Hudson Valley, but up until this time, I had been so busy running my KFC stores and doing regional and national work for KFC, I wasn't involved in my local community.

Paul DeLisio and I had been friends and business associates since he sold me my first insurance policy in the late '60s. After my experience with Jan covertly buying a life insurance policy for me, I realized the value of life insurance, so Paul put together a couple of substantial policies for me. Over the years, as I got more involved in the AKFCF and my national responsibilities, he was building his business and moving up in the world of insurance and financial advising.

Paul and I had "power breakfasts" on a fairly regular basis because we were both interested in the same things. He was president of the board of directors at Benedictine Hospital in Kingston and attended twice yearly Million Dollar Round Table International (MDRT) meetings. He enjoyed hearing about my adventures with the national and regional associations of the KFC franchisees, and I reveled in hearing about his MDRT lectures. We were good buddies who enjoyed similar interests.

Paul recalls our growing friendship this way:

"The Million Dollar Round Table meetings were generally held in the United States, and the five-to-six thousand people who qualified to attend based on their business revenue—they were the top three percent of life insurance people in the world—gathered to learn more about business. There were incredible speakers from every walk of life. I went every year and when I returned to Kingston, I was flying high. It was hard to share my excitement with my wife, Gloria, and the kids," he added. *"They used to tease me, 'C'mon kids, we're going to hear about the MDRT,' but Darlene was very interested. Sharing with each other our mutual excitement in our businesses and what we were learning from the meetings we attended was a natural extension of the socializing the two of us did with our spouses."*

"Darlene was so interesting to me," Paul continues. *"Here's this little gal in Port Ewen who is having these incredible experiences with her travels and working with KFC franchisees all over the country. Compared to me, the majority of her stories were not about local things. My life was right here in Ulster County and a lot of people knew who I was, but not her. It wasn't hard to get to know Darlene, but she just wasn't involved here in Ulster County much before then."*

Like me, Paul had been married, divorced and was now remarried. Wally and I went out for dinner occasionally with Paul and his wife, Gloria, and the four of us had a lot of fun together. Once Paul was in New York City for a national meeting of his industry people at Radio City Music Hall, and Wally and I were having dinner with my accountant, so we invited Paul and Gloria to meet us at the Rainbow Room for dinner.

"Wally was a delightful, welcoming person, and when the four of us went out for dinner, we enjoyed each other's company. I was a young agent, so what could be headier than getting an invitation for dinner and dancing at the Rainbow Room?" Paul recalls. "At the end of the evening, naturally the insurance agent is going to pick up the tab. I had a brand new American Express card and gave it to our waiter. When the waiter returned to say my card didn't go through, Wally said to me, 'This isn't like the Stadium Diner. They don't have time for any baloney. Don't worry about it, Paul,' and he paid. Such a ball buster, how humiliating with one of my top five clients! I paid Wally back, but after that he always called me, 'Hey, Mr. Credit Card!' It was funny. I have a thick skin, so no nightmares."

Darlene and Wally, late 1990s.

DREAM BIG, ADD MOXIE

Nick Pfeiffer's Perspective

From the first time Darlene and I met, we have had a lot in common. I have been a flight attendant since 1976 (work for Delta now), and like her, I always enjoy traveling. She took me on my first cruise—to the Panama Canal in the 80s before they got to be a real big thing—even when she couldn't really afford to do it. She wanted to include me in the experience and she, my dad and I all squeezed into a cabin with bunk beds below the water line. She had gotten divorced from Jan and was deeply in debt, but we had a great time. She and Wally took the two lower bunks, and I got a top bunk.

Later on, when she could afford more lavish cruises, she took us on some really great trips all over Europe and to Russia, Israel, Egypt and lots of other places. We all like to do the same things and always have a lot of fun. When you're a flight attendant, you're always packing and unpacking, but cruises are great because it's like having a traveling hotel room. You only unpack once, and you go to lots of amazing places.

I was raised in Seattle and was out of the house when I was 18. My father, Wally, and my mother moved back to New York where they were from, and we sometimes traveled to Florida to visit an aunt and uncle. I moved down to Fort Lauderdale to study graphic arts and go to art school but I wasn't really into it. My roommate worked as an airline ticket agent and encouraged me to apply. After I worked for Northwest as a ticket agent, I applied to be a flight attendant and moved to Minneapolis. About 20 years ago, my partner, Joey, and I were living in Vancouver when Darlene asked us if we would like to live near her and my father in Florida. We assumed the mortgage on one of Darlene's two condos and Bevy lives across the street. It's like we have our own compound.

My relationship with Darlene is excellent—she's been my mother longer than my real mother, who died in the mid-70s—and most people don't have this kind of relationship

DARLENE L. PFEIFFER

with their mother. We both like traveling, *National Geographic* and animal documentaries, and when she's in Florida in the wintertime, I stop by to see her when I'm out riding my bike. We go out to brunch after church services at Unity, which is a spiritually oriented congregation of people who believe God lives within us. We see eye-to-eye religiously and politically, so there are no big fights at Thanksgiving.

My dad served in Guam as an Air Force meteorologist when the United States bombed Hiroshima. After the war, he went to Alaska to work on the last Aleutian Island. Northwest Airlines wanted him to go to Tokyo in 1950, but they wouldn't pay for my mom's travel and housing, so he quit the airlines and went to work for my uncle who owned Jay Steel on Morton Boulevard in Kingston.

Wally was really good with computers. He had one of the original MacIntosh Apple models and helped Darlene a lot with AKFCF spreadsheets, mailings and graphics in the '80s. Wally, Bevy, my partner Joey and I attended some AKFCF conventions, which we really enjoyed. I especially remember a San Francisco convention when the Colonel's daughter Margaret Sanders was there. Darlene sat at the front with the officers and we all sat at a convention table in the crowd with the franchisees. Margaret was walking through the crowd with a spotlight on her, stopped at our table and said, 'Oh, Nick and Joey! I'm so happy to see you here!' and after that, everyone bought us drinks.

Margaret lived in West Palm Beach and sometimes we had her over for dinner. She had this one crazy Cleopatra outfit and was a lot of fun, like a crazy aunt. Her funeral was the best one I've ever been to—everyone laughed and told stories about her and it wasn't sad at all. She always said, 'I'm livin' off the chicken!' because her father, Colonel Sanders, had left her stores throughout all of Florida when he died. She was an artist and created a sculpture of her father.

Darlene taught me to be on time, or ahead of time, and to never be late. I was never a big planner and she taught me how to plan vacations and my day. She's very regimented, and always writes down goals in her notebook. I used to be day-by-day, but now I'm always thinking about what I've got to do and by when. Darlene is an Auntie Mame type person—she loves to travel and to show you the world. I'm glad she's doing good things with her money, instead of just buying jewelry. Most people don't think so much about others and how they can help them out. I'm very proud of her—she's impressive.

Bevy Hung's Perspective: Part 3

Darlene was just shy of 40 when she got divorced and had gone through a lot. It was a hard time for her, because her relationship with Jan had been very tumultuous. To me, those times defined her and made her more independent as a woman. From then on, she made herself well known in KFC with only three stores, started the magazine and led the franchisees in their lawsuit with PepsiCo.

She has an independent spirit in her, and a wonderful, rare drive to make her own way. She's always trying to be positive, even during hard times—I think it's the mindset of her generation—and it is so inspiring. She didn't get support for running her own businesses from her husband, Jan, but Jake was a great influence. She had innate abilities within her, and Jake helped her take them to the next level by encouraging her and giving her unconditional love.

Darlene used everything she had—she was always savvy about her resources—her intelligence, her beauty, her charm, her intuition about what to say and how to influence others. Those are gifts, and not everyone has them. I teach management classes and one of the things managers always want to learn is how to influence people. For some people, it's like charisma, a quality some naturally possess. Others seek to develop and explore their capacity to be an influencer because they know it's very important. Darlene has that natural ability.

The big thing Darlene taught me was the importance of perseverance: You've got to keep moving forward, keep trying and do the best YOU can do. Don't compare yourself to others. Run your own game. That's very good advice and she exemplifies it. She's competitive and has a lot of confidence in herself, but she grew into that, it evolved over time. When she was moving up at KFC, she had to strengthen that piece of herself, had to be confident and exert herself. She was going to do things in her own way, regardless of whether she was a woman or not. She has struggled but has kept moving forward, a little bit at a time. That's such an important lesson.

Wally was a character—witty, funny, and good for her because he was very confident in himself and she needed a man like that, a man who could be his own person but at the same time, be a great support for her. He was independent in his own way.

They were a good match, compatible. They both served as presidents of the YMCA board and were committed to community service. Wally was handsome and charming too, and a lot of fun. He made the most beautiful cards on the computer, back when few people had computers or knew how to use them creatively. One time he put his head on Michelangelo's naked statue of David and gave it to me. He was very smart, artistic and thoughtful, and he loved his son, Nick. Wally would always want that extra piece of pie, and when Darlene told him he couldn't have it, I'd sneak it to him. I miss him.

CHAPTER 17

The Strength of Family

History offers many lessons to leaders, not the least of which are how to energize and unify group efforts. The best leaders plan ahead and strategize to identify their opponents' weaknesses and strengths, and then assess how to exert positive actions. A healthy dose of bravado and theatrics doesn't hurt, if delivered at crucial moments.

Two years after the Association of Kentucky Fried Chicken Franchisees (AKFCF) formed to unite KFC franchisees and protect and advance our interests, the AKFCF signed a precedent-setting agreement with the Kentucky Fried Chicken Corporation (KFCC). This 1976 Franchise Agreement (also known as the "Magna Carta" of the KFC system) was envied by all other franchisees in the US, as it defined and protected the rights and responsibilities of KFC restaurants across the nation. Subsequent agreements were achieved thereafter—most notably the 1984 memorandum of agreement that regulated ancillary agreements in the system and specified no changes or addenda to the 1976 Franchise Agreement could be made to franchisee contracts without prior review by legal counsel and the National Franchisee Advisory Council (NFAC).

The 1976 Franchise Agreement included very important provisions ("The 4 Ps") which put KFC franchisees in a stronger position than other established franchises such as McDonald's and Burger King. The 4 Ps were royalty rate, ad fee rate, successive renewal and transferability. All of these provisions were directly threatened in the 1980s when PepsiCo purchased KFC and presented the franchisees with their proposal for a new contract. (A 5th provision, protected area, became a big discussion area during another lawsuit in 2007, ultimately resulting in "The 5 Ps.")

The first regional KFC franchisee group formed in the Southeast in 1965 and one started in the Northeast in 1973; as of November 2021, there were seven US KFC franchisee regions. In the beginning, Don Hines, who was a Connecticut franchisee with 14 KFC restaurants, wanted to establish a forum for franchisees to learn from each other and create opportunities for improvement. In 1976, at the initial meeting of the Northeast Franchisee Association in Bermuda, Don was elected president. At my first Northeast regional meeting the following year, Don was stepping down and the vice president refused to take on the duties. No one else would come forward to fill any of the officer positions. Several franchisees asked me if I would serve.

"OK, I'll do it," I said.

In 1978 I became president, vice president, secretary and treasurer of the Northeast AKFCF.

The great thing about being all those officers at once was I didn't have to ask anybody for permission—I could do whatever I thought was best. I had been a president of organizations in high school—the French Club and Future Teachers of America—so I had some knowledge about what it takes to motivate and lead a group of people, but no one would call my experience vast.

I got a shock when I opened our checkbook: The balance was zero, and we owed the National AKFCF $1,500 in membership fees. I learned that although each region operated autonomously, we had to pay the national umbrella association $50 each year per member franchisee. These fees were used to do mailings and to host one national meeting each year. I called Bonnie Shelton, the secretary of the Southeast region to find out what to do.

"How can I get the money?" I asked her. "We don't have a penny."

"Have two meetings—one in the spring and one in the fall—and invite vendors to come," Shelton said. "Provide them with space to show their wares, and then charge them."

After our discussion, I set about fundraising to pay off our debt by inviting vendors to exhibit at our two Northeast regional meetings. The first day-and-a-half-long meeting was held in May of 1978, in Hartford, Connecticut. I charged each vendor $500 to display their wares on card tables (that's all I could afford) set up in the exhibit room of a hotel, and we had a small cocktail party together. That evening, one of the chicken vendors invited me and a group of franchisees to a sit-down dinner in the hotel restaurant. I sat next to Don Hines at a table with two people I had brought from my stores.

"Order very lightly, maybe an appetizer," I whispered to Sheila and Walt. "Just say you're not hungry because I don't have any money to pay for meals." I picked off Don Hines' plate that evening, "Oh, Don, that looks good. Is it?"

"Here, try it," he'd say.

At the end of the evening, much to my surprise, the chicken vendor had picked up the tab for all our meals.

The following day, we convened for presentations before returning to our home bases. That fall, our meeting grew to a two-and-a-half-day event with a full agenda of items we wanted to accomplish. We held it at the Concord Hotel, one of the grand old hotels in the Catskills, and my explicit purpose was for the franchisees and vendors to get to know each other and build camaraderie. We took all our meals together and attended workshops and demonstrations. Vendors set up exhibits in a gymnasium on the premises to feature the filters, cooking equipment, chicken fryers, cash registers and other equipment and supplies we needed to run our stores.

This model served us well and developed into a lucrative, well-attended annual regional convention. During these formative years, all of us gained experience. I learned how to conduct meetings, develop and run our annual convention and, most importantly, attract vendors to it. Eventually, vendors paid $3,000 to exhibit, which allowed us to put funds into our coffers. It took some time, but I finally got our Northeast Region organized, and people came on board to help. Later, this freed me up to say yes when my fellow franchisees asked me to run for office and take on responsibilities at the National Association of KFC Franchisees level.

I can't overstate the networking value of these regional meetings; as our meetings grew in both attendance and length, their purpose solidified. Encouraging and cementing the relationships among franchisees and vendors turned out to be pivotal and doubly important when we entered into legal action against PepsiCo. Having solid partnerships with our vendors saved us a lot of money over the years, and all the goodness that followed grew from those meetings.

The KFCC held its national convention for all the corporate officers, franchisees and vendors each year in February. Those of us who attended these conventions hosted by the corporation would come back very charged up, and I wanted to inspire our managers too.

After one of our national conventions in the early 1980s, I suggested our Northeast regional meetings should highlight the role of the franchise managers and focus on matters of importance to them in their day-to-day operations. I also suggested to the other regional officers we let our store managers know what we had learned. "Let's share that excitement," I said. "Let's turn our spring meetings into managers' meetings."

And that's exactly what we did. We hosted big dinners to honor the managers, and they were a huge success—so much so that Paul Kokalis, regional director of the KFCC franchisees, came to me at the national convention the following year, and said, "We would like to be involved in your regional meetings."

"It's our meeting, Paul, and you are welcome to help me," I replied, "but corporate is not welcome to take it over."

I had realized the value of protecting our most valuable asset—our people and the strength of our network—and I wasn't about to relinquish control to corporate. My instincts were correct: By 1989, when we entered into our epic seven-year lawsuit against PepsiCo, this firm foundation helped us enormously. In these earlier years, none of us knew each other very well yet but as we gradually built trust and formed what became lasting relationships, we created a KFC franchisee family. And it all started with setting up a few card tables for vendors, mingling with each other over cocktails, and enjoying delicious, yet simple, buffet dinners together.

We franchisees always had to juggle our desire to be involved with regional associations with the demands of running our own businesses. When I first went into the business of operating my KFC stores, I naturally thought I would shop around to find the best prices for supplies and equipment. I didn't know the KFC corporate officers demanded franchisees buy from certain suppliers in the 1960s and '70s because the KFCC attached a healthy markup to franchisee prices to insure their own profitmaking.

But, in 1972, a franchisee in Florida successfully sued KFC and achieved the G&K Settlement (the franchisee's name was Garmanthy). Winning that lawsuit decreed we could purchase necessary supplies in the open market, which drastically cut the profit margin corporate had previously enjoyed at our expense. Corporate was disturbed because they made a lot of money from the sales of a wide variety of supplies and equipment, ranging from cash registers to chicken fryers.

In 1979, following on the success of the G&K Settlement, the Southeast Region—always the most progressive, well-established regional association—suggested the AKFCF form the KFC National Purchasing Cooperative to assure we could purchase sustainable, low-cost equipment and supplies from independent sources and, most importantly, corporate could no longer require we buy from their list at a tremendous markup. One of the most enduring traditions of Kentucky Fried Chicken was established by Colonel Sanders himself: He wanted franchisees to function together as a close-knit family and our creation of a strong National Purchasing Cooperative was a natural extension of his beliefs.

In addition to the regional meetings and the National Purchasing Cooperative, the AKFCF and the KFCC established two national committees to further support its work—the

National Franchisee Advisory Committee (NFAC) and the National Advertising Cooperative (NAC)—and I served on both of those too.

The National Purchasing Cooperative formed a board and hired an executive director. Once it was well-established about a decade later, I served as the NAC representative on the cooperative board for a few years. By that time, I could see the man who had been appointed as executive director of the purchasing cooperative was not acting on behalf of the franchisees even though he was our paid employee. Power corrupts, and absolute power corrupts absolutely. Despite the fact that one of my best friends was the chairperson of the board, I could see the executive director had taken complete control of buying, selling, getting vendor contracts and gaining board approval for his actions. No one was really overseeing him, and when I came onto the board, one other woman, Lois Foust, and I began to point out what we were observing. One of my best friends, a yes-man, told Lois and me, "You two can't sit together at our meetings."

"If you want to assign us seats and give us name tags, fine," I replied. "Otherwise, don't tell me where I can sit."

They also told us we weren't allowed to talk with anybody about what was going on with the co-op, which was that the executive director was acting like a king and had established total power. Everyone kept saying, "That's a great idea," no matter what he suggested. Lois and I recognized there was something very wrong going on and remained vigilant.

Every organization needs a separation of powers and oversight, so even when things seem to be running well, you must have the courage to ask questions and raise concerns. The more pushback we got—and the more people said, "Don't upset the apple cart" and "Everything was great until you two came in"—the more I realized the strength of our growing conviction that something was really wrong.

As a representative of the National Advertising Cooperative on the Purchasing Co-op board, my role was to establish a line of communication between the two boards, even though the co-op board tried to get everyone to sign a confidentiality agreement like it was a secret society rather than an organization established to help the franchisees. We finally got the executive director pushed out, though it took some time and he left with a huge golden parachute as payoff for merely doing his job.

When I went to my first National Franchisee Advisory Committee (NFAC) meeting, I was the first woman to be elected to serve on that council. The vice-chairman handed me a pen and said, "Oh great, now that we have a woman, you can take notes."

These were the early days of the second wave of feminism in the United States, but I wasn't involved in or aware of that movement: I was too busy running my own businesses and trying to make them successful. I was driven by a deep desire to get involved in the national AKFCF structure, but couldn't help but notice, right away, women were not on an equal footing with men at these meetings. I had no patience or tolerance for that kind of treatment. I had a very strong gut reaction against what I was observing within the hierarchy of the AKFCF and the KFCC, but it was personal, not political, for me.

"I don't do notes," I said, and handed his pen back to him. "You take the notes if you want notes taken." I don't know where I got that moxie—most women would have taken the pen and begun writing—but not me. Later, I was elected secretary of the NFAC, securing my first role as an officer in the national structure of the AKFCF. My experiences on the regional level had prepared me well to move into higher service on behalf of the franchisees' best interests.

Then, one day, my husband, Wally, was driving us in our car. I was opening our mail when I read a letter that changed the course of my life. This happened just as I was gaining influence and experience on the national level of the AKFCF.

I had been recalled to being a flight attendant for TWA.

DARLENE L. PFEIFFER

It had been proven in Federal Court that TWA had violated our civil rights by not adhering to the provisions in the 1964 Civil Rights Age and Sex Discrimination Act and I now had an unexpected opportunity.

Colonel Jim, Colonel Sanders' nephew, with Darlene.

CHAPTER 18

Securing My Full TWA Pension

Keep your eyes on the prize—even when your eyelids are drooping from sleep deprivation and jet-lag.

When I left flying in 1965 to get married, I had racked up seven years toward my pension, but needed ten, and was barred from continuing to fly because discriminatory practices related to marital status and pregnancy wrongly dismissed women from our jobs. Now, this letter informed me, the class-action lawsuit our union had filed against the airlines in Federal Court had been settled in our favor, and I had a decision to make: Should I return to flying for the next three years? Doing so would allow me to regain my seniority and accrue the full ten years I needed to receive my TWA pension—bringing it from $0 to $50,000 with three more years of flying.

How could I juggle running my businesses and caring for my mother (who was dying at that time), with my growing national responsibilities at the AKFCF? Wally almost drove off the road when I read the letter to him and said I wanted to return to working as a flight attendant.

Wally was shocked, and a little terrified, by my decision because he had been a meteorologist with the airlines in Alaska and attended many riotous off-duty parties. But I hadn't had promiscuous experiences while working for the airlines before and knew I wouldn't now. In 1980, I returned to duty on a full-time basis working three days on and four days off as my schedule permitted.

Those of us who returned to flying were nicknamed "Re-Mos" for "Returning Mothers" by the flight attendants who were already working then. They were upset because we maintained our seniority when we were fired, which meant theirs was reduced and we could gobble up some of the most coveted flights. I'll never forget the advice I received from one of my dear friends, Sherry, a flight attendant who had never left the job: "Don't stand near the open door of the plane," she cautioned. The planes I flew on were 747s, and they were three stories high.

"Why is that, Sherry?"

"Because, Darlene, a lot of the flight attendants don't like those of you who have returned to work," Sherry explained, "and they will push you out the door if they get the chance."

Pearl Nelson, who was the head of the flight attendants' union, was particularly set against us Re-Mos, and one night I called Wally to tell him, "Oh my God! Guess who I'm flying with?" I was so scared to be on a flight with her, but she and I eventually became friends and spent a memorable time together in Rome when she took me all around the city.

For the next three years—while running my KFC stores, tending to my mother's needs as she was slowly dying, and climbing in the ranks of the national AKFCF—whenever I had a flight, I would grab a tuna fish sandwich to eat while driving to Kennedy Airport to catch a red-eye to Paris, Rome, London, Frankfurt, or elsewhere around the globe. I'd touchdown in Europe for 23 hours, catch two hours of sleep, force myself to get up to sightsee and have dinner, then go to bed. At 2:00 a.m. Eastern Standard Time, I would board a return flight to JFK and fly all night. After landing in New York City in the late afternoon, I would drive back up the New York State Thruway to check in at my restaurants before they closed at 9:00 p.m. I was sleep-deprived, but it was worth it.

I was flying nearly every week during those years. The pay was good, and I made back the money I was owed for the years I wasn't allowed to fly, but looking back now, I don't know how I did it! The goal I set for myself made my effort worth it: I regained my full pension and my seniority, and also received passes for flying until TWA merged with American Airlines and its name was retired in 2001.

It was an exciting and demanding time in my life, and

there was one unforeseen and extremely valuable business benefit to flying.

Because of my seniority, I worked in first class, where only the top business executives and internationally renowned celebrities purchased tickets. I had fascinating and instructive conversations with the heads of some of the world's top companies and influencers like Eleanor Roosevelt and Margaret Mead during these overnight trans-Atlantic flights. Those three years of flying provided an unbelievable mentoring experience because conversations with these leaders offered me opportunities to learn from them on what felt like an equal footing. I always dove back into my work at KFC exhilarated, despite being jet-lagged.

CHAPTER 19

Serving KFC Franchisees on a National Level

*Trust builds a solid foundation.
Slow, steady, authentic actions—coupled with knowledge and a
no-nonsense approach—are effective and powerful.*

Meanwhile, back at the AKFCF, whenever new products rolled out, the 13 members of the National Franchisee Advisory Committee (NFAC) would review studies completed by market research groups—and taste test them too—to provide feedback to the company before its products were sold to the public. We took new equipment into a product-testing area to see if it met our standards and we also approved new training programs for franchisees. Depending on who served as the KFC president, corporate often listened to our recommendations and critiques.

I served on the NFAC for about three years as a board member and was also appointed by corporate to serve on an elite committee, the Chef's Council. About 10 of us met every couple of months to taste the newest products and "mystery shop." We visited other chicken franchises—like Popeye's—and talked to the owners about what was involved in running their businesses. Corporate would send us to various cities on a private jet to do our research, which was basically to ask questions and act really dumb to see if we could pick up any secrets or insider tips.

I then turned my attention to the KFC National Advertising Cooperative (NAC). There was a lot of money in our advertising budget because corporate collected two to three percent of each franchisee's gross revenues to create national advertising and public relations campaigns. Compared to the relatively small $100,000 budget of the AKFCF, the power rested with the NAC, which had a budget of about $300 million.

When I first served on the NAC, there were eight franchisees, one franchisee member-at-large and four corporate members, but this was later changed to 13 franchisees and five corporate members. The president of the KFCC was one of the corporate members and always attended the meetings. Although the franchisees had the controlling numbers when it came to a vote, most franchisees went along with whatever the company wanted. I worked my way up to be the NAC's first female chairperson. There was a fair amount of dissention and thick politics on that board and as an executive officer, I could control and influence disputes much more effectively.

Many disagreements emanated from pricing. One of our contractual agreements with corporate was they could not dictate franchisee pricing. However, KFCC's way of controlling our profit margins was to get control of one of the leading KFC products. If they aired an ad for an item at a particular price point, we had to sell it to customers at that price. How could we go up against a price advertised on national TV? That was why it was so important for the franchisees to stick together. A lot of franchisees were afraid of corporate and assumed they would have trouble getting more franchises, for example, but through the years I've learned the importance of standing strong, together.

When I first joined the NAC board, Young & Rubicon, one of the largest and most prestigious advertising agencies in the world, had been KFC's agency for quite some time. One campaign I particularly loved centered on the theme of "Welcome Home to Kentucky Fried Chicken" and was quite poignant. Other popular campaigns included "We serve Sunday dinners seven days a week" and "Get a bucket of chicken, have a barrel of fun." People came into our stores singing the catchy tunes that aired on those TV ads. These campaigns often used images of Colonel Sanders and featured a small child with a homey tagline.

Once each year, NAC members would travel to New York City to see presentations of new advertising campaigns. If we didn't like something, we gave our input, but much of it was ready to roll at that point. Our public relations firm, Daniel J. Edelman Public Relations, was the largest in the world, and they did wonderful work for us. Dan, the owner, and I were good friends and he nicknamed me "the Iron Lady," after British Prime Minister Margaret Thatcher, the first woman to lead a major Western democracy. "You remind me so much of her," he said, and gave me one of the books she wrote.

In my 52 years as a franchisee, there were about 20 different corporate presidents that had to be trained. During the years when I was on the NAC board, the NAC members, Young & Rubicon and the Edelman PR firm worked together well as a team, and everything went along fairly well with our annual campaigns. I would never have permitted anyone to take Y&R or Edelman off as our agencies, but after I went off the board, each newly appointed corporate president insisted on searching for a new advertising agency or PR firm. The NAC members weren't really fighters and asked, "Aren't you happy with Young & Rubican and Edelman?" But since every new president was intent on making a mark, every year or two we had to adjust to working with new advertising and PR companies. Each time, a few months were required to bring on new advertising teams and educate everyone, including the new KFCC president, to our ways. It was hard to run an organization this way, and we lost time and continuity of focus.

As the years passed and corporate takeovers became the norm, corporate owners increasingly viewed KFC as a cash cow and neglected to funnel profits back into the company in favor of selling the entire company at a profit. They wanted to make money, they were going to sell us, and that was that.

This mindset meant franchisees had to be on top of what the company was doing because corporate tried to control the advertising entirely. The franchisees had been the only stabilizing force in KFC, and we provided continuity and oversight as corporate owners came and went.

When I served as the NAC chair, we had to be strong and were often at odds with the company. I formed a group of franchisees who would stick by my side, and one of them, Keith Chambers, owned six KFC's and was co-owner of a larger group that included 36 KFC and Taco Bell restaurants. He became a close friend and a key strategy partner.

"In the 1980s, it was unusual to be a single female on a corporate board, and hold an important responsibility," Keith Chambers said. "The corporation executives would say, 'we are the advertising experts,' and Darlene would say, 'I take offense to that. That is your opinion. I have been in this business longer than you, and I may know things you don't know.' It's like Helen Keller always said, 'Just because a blind person can't see a blue sky, that doesn't mean the sky is less blue.' Darlene had a way of being professional, of positioning her strategic moves in a quiet, classy way, but she'd call 'em on it."

Chambers pointed out the NAC controlled the purse strings on a few hundred million dollars in advertising each year in the 1980s and were established as an independent corporation with paid staff. "Nonetheless," he said, "females had not come of age yet as executives. Some of the 'good ol' boys,' even franchisees, thought a little differently about how to work things out, even though they were good people: They would get things addressed in the men's room. But Darlene would say, 'If you have any more discussions in the men's room, I'm going to be joining you in there.'"

"Darlene was in her 40s then," Chambers added. "I've never known her to be anything but a totally proper lady. She was always a looker, but she always took the high road. Her tenacity—and both of us have that trait—was to take people to task. The two of us would play tag team. We would throw out a line and let them bite, and they would tell us mostly lies and then we would bring them to task. More than a few corporate executives did not know how to handle us," he laughed. "Darlene found other ways around issues when things needed to be fixed. Like Abe Lincoln said, 'If a stump in a field is too big to pull out, you just plow around it and move on, because eventually that stump will just rot.'"

"Darlene had to be one of the first women national franchisees of any brand, perhaps even the first, and against all odds, she overcame any obstacles in her path," Chambers added. "She had tenacity, class, style, professionalism, kept her eye on the big issues, and was a very wise person. I seldom knew her to make fast decisions, but on the other hand, when she encountered integrity problems, she'd move fast—like ripping a Band-Aid off with one yank."

The corporate members on the NAC board weren't concerned about whether or not franchisees made any money from a particular ad. The NAC was producing commercials that cost between $200,000 to $500,000 each and owned the creative rights to them. Corporate offered those ads to marketing firms in China, Korea and Europe to make a profit from selling them. Since corporate members took their profits off the top line, and franchisees made their money off the bottom line, all corporate cared about was getting customers into the stores and taking their royalties from sales. We had to watch to make sure they didn't pull some shenanigans to degrade the KFC franchisees' equity in the NAC or in our store-level profits. Corporate wanted to control the NAC—and later they would, but not at that point. We had to be aware of every ad that aired on national television so each KFC restaurant could make a profit.

There were often deep-rooted debates regarding strategic branding versus price point tactical promotions. National advertising campaigns frequently promoted special offers that weren't cost-effective for the franchisee. It was often true that a customer would come into our store specifically because they had seen, for example, a $5 KFC box advertised on TV featuring two pieces of chicken, biscuit, potatoes, gravy and a soda. We had to push the box, but there was no way to make money on it and no chance to upgrade it. We always had to have whatever had been promoted, even if we didn't make money on it. If we raised concerns or complained, corporate would just say, 'You'll make it up in volume,' as they skimmed their percentage of our gross revenues to fund the next advertising campaigns. We had to raise the prices on our other boxes to $5.39 so we could make a little money, while still offering the one $5 box advertised on TV.

I realized if the franchisees let corporate completely control the advertising campaigns and budgets—and didn't exercise the control they had on the NAC—corporate would continue to eat into the franchisees' profits. The franchisees made money from their bottom line, but corporate made their profits from skimming off our top line. That's why it was so important to maintain control of what corporate was doing whenever we could.

One of the KFCC presidents was Peter Waller, from Australia, and I loved him. He served while I was head of the NAC and the executive director and I had developed a plan to control a portion of the advertising dollars to be more beneficial to the franchisees. I let Peter conduct an hour-long counter-presentation on a NAC telephone conference call one day. He finished and asked if I wanted to call for a vote, but I told him what I already knew before he'd started: we didn't have a quorum. I used the telephone to the franchisees' advantage, and when Peter left his presidency, he gave me a sterling silver Tiffany's telephone key chain in recognition of my strategic move that day. I still have that Tiffany's telephone.

I earned a reputation as a committed hard worker, and people could see I was not easily convinced to just go along, but rather that I was assertive and willing to fight for what I believed was the best interest of franchisees. After I had proven myself in the Northeast regional group, as well as in positions of responsibility in both of these two national committees, the franchisees asked me to serve on the national board of the AKFCF.

I worked my way up from second vice president to first vice president and in 1988, I became the first woman chosen to serve as president of the Association of Kentucky Fried Chicken Franchisees; in 1995, I served as president again, becoming the first person to serve two terms as AKFCF president. As AKFCF president, I automatically had a seat on the National Advertising Council too.

(L to R): Bob Peck, a former AKFCF president; Darlene; Andy Selden, legal counsel during PepsiCo lawsuit.

CHAPTER 20

PepsiCo Takes Ownership of KFC

*Complacency is dangerous. Expect the unexpected.
Uncover as many facts as possible before signing agreements.
One good starting point is understanding, and then protecting,
your rights.*

In 1986, when PepsiCo purchased KFC from R. J. Reynolds for $840 million, we had no sense of foreboding because we had become accustomed to corporate take-overs. The Colonel had first sold KFC to Massey/Brown, who then sold it to Heublein, followed by R.J. Reynolds and then PepsiCo.

Although many people think of colored sugar water when they hear PepsiCo, it was already a very robust and diverse company with several businesses and products, including Lay's and Frito Lay. But one thing distinguished the PepsiCo corporate structure from KFC: The PepsiCo business model was based upon distribution. We didn't know that when they first took over KFC but discovered during the lawsuit that they assumed they would augment their business model by adding Kentucky Fried Chicken to their distribution chain.

However, they did not realize how strong our franchise agreements, including five provisions—which we called The 5 Ps—were, or how vital territorial protections were to our franchisees' success.

PepsiCo also did not realize we sold our chicken based on one important, traditional selling point: fresh, never frozen. PepsiCo didn't realize how hard we would fight to preserve that. They were used to being in the distribution business, but we were in the restaurant business. We, in turn, didn't realize PepsiCo's purpose in trying to change our contract was to take our territorial rights away from us.

We later learned the value of these territorial rights, but none of this was clear to us at the outset. We only knew one thing: we needed to protect the franchisees' territorial rights.

Once PepsiCo took over KFCC, the AKFCF needed to hire a new lawyer because ours, who also represented Frito Lay, a division of PepsiCo, had a conflict of interest. Bob Schlutz (AKFCF president), Dick Hines and I did an attorney search on behalf of the AKFCF board of directors, separately interviewing four candidates, and then comparing notes. We mutually agreed Andy Selden, a highly recommended Minneapolis attorney who specialized in franchise law, was our best choice.

Those who took on the AKFCF presidency rotated in succession from the various regions around the country, but I never set out to serve in that role. However, I had been so actively involved and instrumental in the development of my region, and on the national committees, that when it came time for our Northeast Region members to nominate a president, they asked me to fulfill the duties. I said I would, with my main goal being to continue to be of service to the franchisees. Andy had been working with us for six months by the summer of 1988 when I began my first one-year term as AKFCF president.

In February 1989, the franchisees were officially notified PepsiCo was determined to unilaterally change our longstanding 1976 Franchise Agreement and our 1984 Memorandum of Agreement. Several of the PepsiCo proposals were unfavorable to franchisees, but one of the worst clauses would have meant chicken could be prepared in commissaries throughout the country, frozen, and then shipped to grocery stores for direct sales to the public, cutting the franchisees out of the picture. This was onerous and would have put us all out of business—but we didn't grasp the ramifications of what they were trying to accomplish until later.

When we first received the proposed contract changes, the franchisees thought PepsiCo wanted to gain the right to put stores wherever they wanted. Their proposed contract changes included removal of The 4 P's and the end of franchisees' territorial protections based on population and radius. The latter provision outlined there could be only one store within whichever measurement was smaller: 30,000 population or 1.5-mile radius. For instance, if a franchisee had a store producing a million dollars in gross or topline revenues, PepsiCo could put another store directly across the street, effectively creating a market to support two $500,000 stores instead of a single million-dollar store. Their proposed contract alterations also specified this provision couldn't be changed without the full understanding of the NFAC. However, a key part of this change was that corporate interpreted "understanding" to be construed as "just being presented" rather than proposed changes being discussed, then agreed to or amended. This issue became a key point in our lawsuit and part of the settlement, which then created a new agreement known as The 5 P's.

John Cranor, president of PepsiCo, came to see me and slammed a new contract down in front of me and very bluntly said, "You have to accept this new contract! You'll have to work with me!"

I had no idea what was in it, so I said, "We're not accepting it."

"Look, little lady, I can do anything I want," he retorted angrily, "and you don't have anything to say about it. You'll either accept this contract or else you'll have to deal with me."

He was very formidable in his suit and horn-rimmed glasses.

I looked at him demurely, and said, "Well, I guess you'll have to deal with me," standing my ground with a smile.

The very next day, one of the franchisees flew us in his private jet to Louisville, Kentucky, which was where the PepsiCo and KFCC corporate offices were located, and the AKFCF filed a lawsuit in federal court to protect our interests on our previously negotiated terms.

The main points of vulnerability for the franchisees during the lawsuit centered on five provisions or as we called them, The 4 P's plus Paragraph 19 (which covered protected radius), all of which PepsiCo wanted to eliminate or drastically

change in unbeneficial ways. They were:
- *Territorial protection* (outlined in Paragraph 19): PepsiCo wanted to eliminate this protection. Our original contract stated franchises must be spaced at least 1.5 miles apart or serve a population area of at least 30,000 people, whichever was smaller, with any change made "with the understanding of the NFAC." Franchisees took this to mean "negotiated in good faith," but the judge ruled against that, unfortunately.
- *Right of succession*: Franchisees could pass on their stores to their heirs, but PepsiCo wanted to specify conditions—such as how much money the successor had in the bank and breadth of business experience—for successions to occur. In other words, we could not just give our businesses to our children.
- *Royalty rate*: This fee, which franchisees paid to KFCC, covered the cost of doing business and was set in writing at four percent. PepsiCo wanted to raise it to five percent or leave it open ended.
- *Ad fee rate*: The ad fee rate was set at three percent of the franchisees' gross revenue and PepsiCo wanted to raise this rate as well. Franchisees did not want to raise it because we commonly gave an additional 1.5 percent of gross revenue to local advertisers and wanted to be able to afford to retain that expenditure. If royalty fees and ad fees were raised by corporate, franchisees' profits would be adversely affected: Corporate wanted to skim off our gross receipts, but franchisees made their profits off the bottom line.
- *Transferability*: If a franchisee wanted to sell their business to someone outside of their family, PepsiCo wanted to control these transfers and have the ability to qualify, and potentially refuse, them.

With battle lines drawn, we immediately began to strategize about how to set into motion what became an eight-year fight, much of it conducted with me at the helm. Andy Selden was a godsend: He knew his way around franchise law and was a brilliant strategist.

With just $20,000 in our AKFCF treasury—not nearly enough to go up against a giant corporation like PepsiCo—the first thing we had to figure out was how to raise the money for legal fees.

The beauty of what happened over the next eight years was the franchisees were already bonded together as a family, and we understood the value of sticking together to negotiate in our collective best interests.

My husband Wally and my friend Paul DeLisio were both amazed at what we were doing. "Here she was, a little franchisee living in Kingston with three stores, going up against a big corporation," Paul recalled. "The beauty of their plan was that the franchisees stuck together."

Wally told me, "Darlene, what you're doing is crazy. You're like a little bug on the sidewalk to PepsiCo, and they can snuff you out, just like that." I said, "If I die, it will be for my fellow franchisees." I became like Joan of Arc. Wally and Paul both thought PepsiCo would retaliate against me and take away my stores, but I decided to fight.

Keith Chambers explained my way of thinking this way: "Part of Darlene's overarching strategy to protect her personal business was to build a great KFC at home, so corporate couldn't come after her, for going into default or for any other chink in her armor. She had well-paid management at her stores and was always one of our better operators," he explained. "She wouldn't be compromised because her home operations were always strong and she gained more credibility from other franchisees as a result. She spent extra money to have stronger people at home so she could be out there fighting on behalf of the franchisees."

But before we could take action, franchisees all over the United States needed to grasp the danger of our situation, learn what we planned to do about it and unite, so Andy

DARLENE L. PFEIFFER

Selden and I flew around to each of the eight regional meetings. We had no other way to communicate the gravity of our situation except phone calls and our campaign to win the lawsuit required personal interaction and discussion with many franchisees at once. At the regional meetings, I explained how much money each store would need to raise and asked them to contribute. I impressed upon them we had to act, decisively, so we could protect our rights.

Once the majority of franchisees signed on to the lawsuit, they became more supportive and involved. It hadn't been easy to convince them, and I knew we had to continue to communicate, often and deeply, to keep them engaged. But how?

Group shot of several past AKFCF presidents and others at a convention workshop. Darlene's presentation focused on the AKFCF Quarterly Magazine.

CHAPTER 21

Capturing the Printing Presses

Get inspiration from history and lessons learned by successful people. Keeping an icon or affirmation in mind can give you strength when you need it most.

In 1980, a mimeographed eight-page newsletter was initiated to disseminate regional meeting minutes and other information of value to the franchisees. Three years later, we established the first comprehensive, region-by-region franchisee mailing list; between this simple newsletter and our mailing list, we were doing what we could to stay in touch with franchisees. Keep in mind, this was before email and the Internet.

But by the late 1980s, I knew we needed to rachet up our communication a few notches and I wanted to create a magazine. Once the lawsuit against PepsiCo was underway, we had to forcefully and directly convey information to the franchisees. I called Bonnie Shelton again at the Southeast Region because she had published an excellent history of their region's development and I asked her who had written it. She referred me to Webb Howell, a fine writer and publisher in North Carolina.

Webb and I, along with the executive committee of the AKFCF, transformed the newsletter into the *AKFCF Quarterly Magazine*, a glossy, four-color publication funded by full page ads from our vendors. Publishing a professionally produced magazine paid for by advertisers opened up opportunities to develop unique content, use more photography, and print in full color, which few franchisee organizations were doing at that time. It became one of the most important tools we used to inform and engage the franchisees, and its value cannot be underestimated.

While we were flying around the country talking with

franchisees about the lawsuit, I drew inspiration from Joan of Arc and the rebels who fought in the French Revolution. One of the first things the rebels did was capture the press and I kept the image of Joan of Arc riding fearlessly into battle as my personal guiding icon.

We didn't have a printing press to capture like Joan of Arc did, but I knew the *AKFCF Quarterly Magazine* was the best way to inspire and galvanize our troops. As Howell said of me, "Darlene had a vision for what the publication could be and was willing to let us write stories that were provocative."

As the publication's first editor, I wanted to make a strong statement. One of the early covers displayed a pair of hands bound by handcuffs emblazoned with this headline from the feature article, "Franchisees: Slaves or Indentured Servants?" Over the next few years under my editorial leadership, the magazine served as a cohesive force to strengthen the KFC franchise system. I worked with Webb about 10 years, and we accomplished a lot together.

Webb Howell produced publications for many restaurant and franchise groups over the decades and brought a deep understanding of the issues involved in the franchisees' lawsuit against PepsiCo. The KFC franchisees hired their PR firm, Edelman, to study meal occasions. Another thing Howell understood was the value of each franchisee's commitment to uniformity.

"One store has a tremendous impact on all units," Howell explained. "A couple years ago, I was in Florence, Italy, and ate at a McDonald's at the train station. It was essentially the same food as I would get here in the U.S. and was great comfort food in a place where I didn't speak the language. Franchises cook to a standard no diner can meet with certainty, and KFC franchises created a lot of uniformity. Corporate KFC didn't care about those standards, and just wanted to milk money out of the organization.

"One of the things that's really unique about the KFC franchise group," Howell continued, "is when a chain starts, the owner usually goes into it with the recipe, a business model, branding, and all the pieces in place. But Harland Sanders didn't have any of that stuff. The franchisees created the brand, they cared about it, and they have always believed they were the brand—and because of this, they were enormously possessive of that brand. KFC had been traded around like baseball cards, treated as a cash cow, because it was popular, a great product. PepsiCo wanted to take the brand and spread it around in different ways. They didn't care if it was sold in restaurants, grocery stores or wherever, and the lawsuit was basically about the franchisees maintaining territorial control. Colonel Sanders hadn't really thought that through, but his franchisees had a tremendous sense of entitlement about the brand.

"Darlene brought a lot of intelligence to the lawsuit," Howell added. "She is one of the truly special people I've worked with over the years. I didn't really appreciate what it took to accomplish what she did back then. She was clearly qualified, a very dynamic and generous person. I just accepted she was great at what she did, AND she's a woman. My appreciation has grown over the years. Darlene's personality lends itself toward a survivor and she is enormously upbeat, all quite important things. We would talk through our editorial decisions, decide what was important, make a plan, and things went smoothly because she knew where she could make a contribution, and when to delegate."

Howell added perspective on running a KFC restaurant, too. It takes about 30 employees to run a restaurant, all of them working different shifts, and since I was running three restaurants, that meant supervising and training 100 employees. As the franchise business model progressed over the years, people eventually moved into management positions but back then, franchisees relied upon employees who were high school students, many of whom were embarking upon their first jobs. They required training and nurturing because you're dealing with kids. "It takes an enormous amount of training and positive reinforcement to make your business successful," Howell pointed out. "Your employees are always part of your bottom line."

Howell also understood how demanding it can be to move on several different fronts at once. "Darlene was always a really great multitasker. She had stores in New York, and she lived in both New York and Florida. How do you run an organization like that? You have to be enormously organized," he noted. "One thing about Darlene was you wanted to work hard for her. You didn't want to disappoint her, even though she would be the first person to let you off the hook. I won't say it was easy to please her—she was not willing to take second best—but we never had a disagreement. She was enormously accepting of others' ideas. I remember her saying 'There's nothing I wouldn't do for my employees and nothing they wouldn't do for me; that's just the way it is,' and people always felt heard. Giving people room to have their say diffused a lot of potential trouble."

As editor of the *AKFCF Quarterly Magazine*, Howell and I worked together very productively and positively. Howell recalled, "Darlene was very plugged into the issues. She set the tone for the magazine, knew what was going on, and even advertisers were picking it up. She was in the catbird seat all the time. She had the courage and understood how far, and when, to push. During the heat of the battle, from 1989 until the end of the lawsuit in 1997, she knew what to do and when to do it. I don't think another person could have done what she did. She's had significant accomplishments in business and many other things, and she got ahead at a time when it was hard to do for a woman. But she didn't wave a flag. She just worked at it, was nice to people and made everybody feel good. That's a rare thing," he said. "She didn't need social media, didn't toot her own horn, was not on top of people, that's not her. Darlene has a personality that makes you want to be friends with her, and she makes an effort to stay in touch."

CHAPTER 22

Building a War Chest for the Battle with PepsiCo

*Challenges often bring opportunities.
Remain open and alert to the potential for good outcomes.*

Two months after we filed the lawsuit, KFCC refused at the last minute to sponsor the annual KFC convention slated to be held in Las Vegas, a twist no one anticipated.

John Cranor, PepsiCo's president, spoke to me like I was a petulant child. "If you're going to sue us, I'm taking away your convention," he said. "We spend a lot of money every year on a convention for you unappreciative franchisees."

This turned out to be a fortuitous development. When I went back to our group to discuss it, we decided to do the convention ourselves. The esprit de corps of working and being together was the most important strength of our franchisee group—and we knew it.

That's when we started to run our own convention. We had no money for a convention in Las Vegas, but I got a break for us on rooms at a Marriott Hotel in Florida. Since we had no convention planning team, my husband, Wally, and I sat down at our kitchen table and hand-addressed all the invitations. It was a dramatic step down but it was the only way I could keep the convention once Cranor dropped his bombshell in my lap.

Looking back, I can see the universe was working with us. The lawsuit was all-consuming, as were our efforts to raise funds for our legal team, but more than 500 franchisees and guests attended our first AKFCF-sponsored national convention in Florida, which served us well at a critical time as both a networking and fundraising event. What could have been the franchisees' greatest setback became one of our greatest successes: Years later, when we were able to hire a convention planner, I saw our first convention was a major turning point.

I did not have money to hire a keynote speaker, so I invited Margaret Sanders, the Colonel's daughter, to address our group. She was a dynamic speaker and the perfect choice for the times. As a little girl, Margaret had taste-tested her father's Kentucky Fried Chicken recipe while he was developing it in the early years, and she had witnessed his tenacity, hard work and success. She also knew how important the basic foundation of treating all the franchisees and vendors like they were family had been to her dad: Keeping our family of franchisees and vendors together ultimately attracted exactly what we needed to win the lawsuit.

Margaret set our world on fire that day: "Daddy loved you guys," she boomed in her clear, Southern-tinged accent, "and I love you too. Don't you let that damn corporation kick you around!"

She got a standing ovation, and we raised a lot of money for our lawsuit. All the groundwork we had laid over the years to build relationships with our vendors and amongst ourselves paid off. What Cranor envisioned as a punishment—removing corporate support for our annual convention—became a rallying cry to inspire our family of franchisees and vendors to unite and we ultimately attracted the support we needed for our lawsuit.

"Going forward, we decided we would do the convention ourselves every year," said Keith Chambers. "When I was AKFCF president, we brought in Brooks & Dunn, who had just won a bunch of Grammy Awards, and bestselling author, Mitch Albom, as keynote speaker. Contrary to what corporate had told us—they claimed they never made money on the convention—we discovered it was a BIG moneymaker and they made six or seven figures every year from the convention. This provided us with the legal bullets needed to fund the lawsuit. It was one of the most clever things, and we actually did it by accident."

"The AKFCF didn't have money until we took over the convention," Chambers added. "We were the first franchisee brand to control the national convention, and other franchisee groups have since done the same thing."

> **The Hard Way**
>
> *By Colonel Sanders*
>
> It is comparatively easy to prosper by trickery, the violation of confidence, oppression of the weak . . . sharp practices, cutting corners—all of those methods that we are so prone to accept and do as "business shrewdness."
>   It is difficult to prosper by the keeping of promises, the deliverance of value in goods, in services, and in deeds—and in the meeting of so called "shrewdness" with sound merit and good ethics.
>   The easy way is efficacious and speedy—the hard way arduous and long. But, as the clock ticks, the easy way becomes harder, and the hard way becomes easier.
>   And as the calendar records the years, it becomes increasingly evident that the easy way rests hazardously upon shifting sands, whereas the hard way builds solidly a foundation of confidence that cannot be swept away.

CHAPTER 23

A Second Term as President and the Final Push to Success

Stay calm and stay the course.

The lawsuit against PepsiCo went on for eight years until it was resolved in 1997, but by the mid-1990s, negotiations were so mired we couldn't get things moving.

Someone said, "Get Darlene back. We need her leadership. She'll get stuff settled!" and nominated me to the presidency. At the 1995 convention, I agreed to serve again, becoming the only AKFCF president to serve twice.

The lawsuit was a long, laborious slog for me, especially because I was running my own businesses and serving on the National Advertising Council as well. We had a law firm in Louisville, Kentucky—Wyatt, Terrant and Combs—and of course we always had Andy Selden, our stalwart attorney, who led the way in countless meetings and worked hand-in-hand with our law firm to strategize next steps.

I wrote regular letters to the franchisees to update them about the progress of the lawsuit, which made David Novak, president of the KFCC, furious. He stormed into one of our franchisee meetings uninvited, waving one of my letters above his head. Then he tore it up, threw it on the floor right in front of everyone, and stomped on it, yelling, "I'm sick and tired of you franchisees making a fool of me! You franchisees are making me look crazy."

As he stood there angry and panting from his outburst, I eyed him calmly and said, "Mr. Novak, I never thought of you as a fool or as crazy, but you're doing a really good job of making yourself look like a fool right now, all without my help."

"I'm not staying here," he said, and stomped to the door, where he stood looking at us, waiting.

"Oh, Mr. Novak, don't go away mad," one of the franchisees called out.

After a long pause, a deep-voiced franchisee who owned one single store, said "Let him go. Let him go," from the back of the room.

When the lawsuit with PepsiCo was finally settled, the franchisees won on the most important provision: retaining our right of territorial control. This assured us retention of our rights and became The 5th P. This win became even more impressive when we discovered, after the settlement, PepsiCo had planned to establish regional commissaries where they would cook and freeze chicken to sell directly to supermarkets.

The settlement also specified the merger of the previous NAC and the NFAC into one committee, a win-win for both the corporation and the franchisees. The newly formed National Council and Advertising Coop (NCAC) increased franchisee membership from eight to 13, and corporate from four to five members, which allowed franchisees to retain complete control of the decisions made by the NCAC. It was also easier for everyone involved to deal with just one committee.

Said Chambers: "Darlene is a perfect example of a service-based leader, like Mother Theresa. There's nothing so infectious as a good example. She believes—and lives—the idea of 'giving is living and living is giving' more than any other person I've known in my life. I've heard her tell people one way to achieve immortality is to give, and she set examples with both words and deeds. As she put it, 'Well done is better than well said,' and in thirty years of working together, we saw a lot of that from her.

"Darlene made me a better person. A lot of people are good at fighting," Chambers added, "but to actually get results? That's another thing. She would always find a way to get to 'yes' because she is a lady of class, tenacity and style."

A photograph taken to culminate the settling of the lawsuit features me as AKFCF president, Keith Chambers as NAC

DARLENE L. PFEIFFER

president, John R. Neal and Bob Peck [two influential franchisees who were also named, along with me, when the lawsuit was filed], and David Novak, president of Tricon, the company that eventually became YUM [and took over KFC from Pepsi-Co]. We were signing documents outside the Ritz Carlton at Laguna Nigel, California, with the Pacific Ocean as backdrop to symbolize our peaceful intentions.

1998 PepsiCo - KFC lawsuit settlement signing. Seated (L – R): Fred Baeur, chairman, NFAC; Keith Chambers, chair, NAC. Standing (L – R): David Novak, YUM! Inc.; Bob Peck, AKFCF Steering Committee; Darlene Pfeiffer, president, AKFCF; Donald Parkinson, senior vice president, KFC Franchising; John R. Neal, AKFCF Steering Committee.

CHAPTER 24

Giving Is Eternal— The KFC Scholarship Program

The more we care about others, the more we give to others, the happier we are. Everything we give comes back to us.

I'm a long-time believer in educational scholarships, and I learned how to create and develop them during my years at Kentucky Fried Chicken.

In 2000, I owned three KFC franchises in Kingston and Poughkeepsie, and was vice chairperson of the Kentucky Fried Chicken National Council and Advertising Coop (NCAC), established as a result of our successful lawsuit against Pepsi-Co. That year, KFC and the NCAC created the Colonel Sanders Kentucky Fried Chicken Scholarship Program, a public relations effort to show KFC was helping people in communities throughout the United States.

For the first few years, the program awarded $20,000 scholarships in each of the eight KFC regions and funded them solely from contributions from all KFC stores. Each store contributed four cents per pound of the coleslaw they bought from the KFC National Purchasing Cooperative. The number of scholarships awarded was directly tied to the amount of coleslaw purchased: This total figure, divided by $20,000, determined the number of scholarships awarded each year.

An executive director, Cindy Harbin, was hired to uphold our stringent standards for the selection of scholars, and Cindy and I and one other franchisee would fly to the American College Testing (ACT) headquarters in Iowa to help choose the KFC Scholarship winners. Each year, we reviewed about 1,000 nationwide applications which had been pre-selected by the ACT. With intense competition nationwide, very few franchisees were able to award scholarships to students living in their local communities. Imagine how many aspiring college students lived in the Northeast region, which stretched from Maine to Virginia, and then realize only about five students from that entire region could receive a scholarship. The competition for this small number of $20,000 scholarships was quite fierce.

The amazing diversity of the student applicants, and their backgrounds and aspirations impressed me. Each of the eight regions of our country had its own idiosyncrasies and a distinct culture—for example, there were many Vietnamese students living in southern California—and I learned a lot about how different our country's regions were from being a part of this selection process.

Public service was one central component of the applicant evaluation process, but applications from Midwest students who lived in farming communities showed very little volunteerism or community service. These students woke up early, did chores, attended school, came home to do chores again, did homework and went to bed. We soon realized the demands of their lifestyle left little time for them to sell poppies for veterans, read to seniors at a nursing home or even help create a float for their town's Memorial Day parade. Outside of school hours, these students were busy helping their families survive by milking the cows, weeding crops in the fields, and mucking out barn stalls.

After about four years of doing this joyful work, I broached the subject: "Why can't we have some direct input and participation from the franchisees?"

I was driven by my memory of how I felt when I applied for and received a college scholarship. It gave me the financial support I needed to achieve my goals and made a lasting impact on me as a young woman who was building confidence. It changed my life for the better, no doubt about it.

I had come to realize individual franchisees weren't involved enough in the Colonel Sanders KFC Scholarship Program, nor aware of its impact on the families living in their communities. I believed if the franchisees could be directly involved in expanding our scholarship program, they would reap community-building benefits, expand their customer base, gain control over how many students received scholarships in their region and share the joy of giving locally.

The most significant benefit of creating more scholarships, beyond good public relations, was to the high school students who would receive these funds. If franchisees could contribute $10,000 toward a local KFC Scholarship to be awarded within their own region—and the KFC Foundation matched this contribution 50/50—the number of $20,000 KFC Scholarships designated for each region would dramatically increase.

I had learned about donor-directed funds from another board I served on, so I mapped out a plan. I suggested franchisees' contributions to a donor-directed scholarship fund would be matched, 50:50, to expand the Colonel's Scholarship Fund. Funding for these scholarships was kept separate from those funded by the "coleslaw contributions," and franchisee contributors could target a city or high school and encourage scholars in their local communities to apply. To me, this was very important because it would bring the community and the franchisees closer, while benefiting students from local families. Since the program was close to home, everyone would be more involved in the process. Students who received the scholarships were invited to attend a ceremony and a meal at the local KFC store, and their families came too, which was a great way for franchisees to build community good will and relationships.

Step one was to have the Colonel Sanders KFC Scholarship Foundation Board approve my concept and formally initiate a donor-directed scholarship category. This would allow corporate employees, vendors and especially franchise owners to contribute from $5,000 to $10,000 and have their contribution matched by the foundation. Scholarship recipients would then be selected from student applicants from the city or high school where franchises were located.

DARLENE L. PFEIFFER

The foundation board expressed initial resistance to my ideas to expand the program, but I waged a relentless campaign to counter their reluctance and, with a lot of lobbying and input from many lifelong friends and associates, I prevailed. If a franchisee anywhere in the United States contributed (as little as $5,000 and up to a maximum of $10,000), the KFC Scholarship Foundation Board of Directors would match it, dollar for dollar.

Beginning a month prior to our 2004 national convention in New Orleans where the program announcement and fundraising campaign would officially kick off, I kept the pressure on. By the time the convention's opening day arrived, I had secured a prominent spot on the agenda for the general session to give a brief report about this new initiative and how it would benefit the KFC corporation and the franchisees.

Prior to this official presentation, I arranged to discuss the expanded scholarship program at each of the eight regional franchisee meetings held at the convention. I wanted to familiarize the franchisees and our KFC suppliers with the new concept and when I approached them to see if they were interested in participating, they enthusiastically accepted.

The schedule for our annual convention was always tightly packed and set months in advance but I asked for a coveted last-minute spot on the agenda at the 2004 convention. I wanted to address everyone to get buy-in for the expanded scholarship program, and the conference organizers quickly agreed: Everyone knew and respected me for my leadership role in the successful lawsuit the KFC franchisees had won against PepsiCo in 1997.

Just as I was about to give my main platform presentation, Keith Chambers, then the president of the Association of KFC Franchisees (AKFCF) and my convention co-chair, asked me if I would mind following our keynote speaker, Mitch Albom, the author of *Tuesdays With Morrie*, who had a plane to catch. I agreed, which was a fortuitous re-scheduling.

As we listened to Mitch tell several heartwarming stories

of his own transformation and Morrie's incredible courage and generous spirit, my partner, Paul DeLisio, whispered to me, "Darlene, you could raise a million dollars right here today. You could get fifty commitments of ten thousand dollars each, with the foundation matching all of them to raise another five hundred thousand."

That gave me the encouragement I needed. I had never considered raising a million at the convention, but now I had incentive and confidence.

I began to picture how it could be done.

The story Mitch told as he concluded his speech really inspired me. When Morrie was very near the end of his life, Mitch told us, he bounded up the steps for their weekly visit and asked, "How's it feel to be dying?"

Morrie, who could barely raise his head, looked at him and said, "I'm not dying. As long as I'm giving, I'm living."

No one could have asked for a better warm-up act. Mitch Albom left the stage to thunderous applause as I walked up to the microphone.

I waited for the crowd to settle and launched into my overview of the program. I positioned an expansion of the Colonel Sanders KFC Scholarship Fund as an opportunity for us to double the impact of a well-established program. Even better, we would be assured that scholarships would be awarded to students selected from each of the regions where our KFC stores operated. There would be one scholarship for every $10,000 a franchisee contributed, and each of the franchisees would present a $20,000 scholarship at the time and place of their choice.

The high pitch of altruism ignited by Mitch's speech inspired me to be bold. I took the microphone into my hands and began pacing the stage, pointing and calling out the names of the corporate president and other executives.

"How about you, Mr. Brown? How much are you going to contribute to this fund? Will you be the first contributor?"

"Yes, I'll do five scholarships at $10,000 a piece," he said.

"I'll contribute $50,000."

I was shameless. After Mr. Brown responded positively, so did each of the others I called out by name. One by one, corporate executives and national vendors each committed $10,000. As the excitement built, franchisees stood up—most of whom were my personal friends—and committed to contributing too.

It was exhilarating for everyone present.

When I left the stage, I had enough verbal commitments from the corporation presidents, executives, vendors and the franchisees to feel confident I could hit my goal of $1 million dollars before the convention ended the next day. But my work was not done yet. I spent the next hours raising the rest of the funding at parties, meetings, workshops and even the breakfast session on the final day.

Nobody wanted to see me coming towards them because they knew it would cost them $10,000.

"How about you, Jim? Don't you want to be one of the people who made this happen?"

Bingo, I had them, each and every one I approached.

I was relentless.

At the closing session of the conference, I took the stage once more to announce we would kick off the new scholarship program with fifty $20,000 scholarships, funded by $500,000 from the regional franchisees and matched, 50:50, by $500,000 from the KFC Scholarship Foundation board of directors.

I had raised a million dollars in three days.

Telling this story is one of my favorite ways to inspire people to give whenever I deliver a motivational talk.

When we first expanded the Colonel Sanders KFC Scholarship Program that year, fifty $20,000 scholarships were awarded, but as it grew, hundreds of regional scholarships were awarded each year.

Several Ulster and Dutchess County students received these Colonel Sanders KFC Scholarships. Each year, I selected one local high school to compete for the scholarship and I always invited the scholarship recipient and their family to attend a chicken dinner and award ceremony at one of my KFC restaurants so I could meet them in person.

In the summer of 2018, I was having dinner at Christina's Restaurant in Kingston when a woman came over to my table and said, "Are you Darlene Pfeiffer? I'm Sean Alvarez's mother."

"I'm so glad to see you! How's Sean doing?"

Eleven years before, Sean had become the first recipient of the Colonel Sanders KFC Scholarship in Ulster County. His family lived in Saugerties and he had a twin brother. I remembered both of these young men and their dreams of working in law enforcement.

"He's a DEA Agent living in Puerto Rico," his mother said, proudly. "He's married and his wife is a nurse. He's doing great!"

"That's wonderful. I'm very happy to hear this. Please tell Sean I said hello."

This chance encounter with Sean's mother reminded me that what we do for each other really matters.

Expanding the Colonel Sanders KFC Scholarship Program helped many young people achieve their goals. This program is a shining example of my belief that when you give, you live eternally.

My appreciation for Mrs. Fleming, who gave me a boost when I really needed one, drove my dedication to help support students later in my life. Receiving and giving are two sides of the same coin: When you pay it forward, everyone benefits and, of course, when you give, you live eternally. When you do something for another person, it's not just about the mere act of whatever you gave. Giving can inspire profound changes in someone's life, even though you may never know the long-term impact of your gift.

This KFC scholarship program still exists, though it has changed dramatically. Today, these scholarships are offered solely to college students who are KFC employees, whereas earlier, franchisees could direct the scholarships to the general public and students from their local high school were invited to apply. When originally conceived, this program was a win-win for the scholarship recipients as well as for Kentucky Fried Chicken: It helped raise the corporate profile, established KFC as an integral community member, and was beneficial to students aspiring to attend college. Today, it remains a vital initiative and continues to change lives.

The people you give to now will outlive you, and however you give will influence their lives. That's so important.

I believe that when we give, we live more fully.

When we give, we live completely.

When we give, we live more joyously.

And, when we give, we live eternally.

Or, as Morrie put it, "As long as I'm giving, I'm living."

Anreka Gordon:
Colonel Sanders KFC Scholarship Winner

Anreka Gordon graduated from Poughkeepsie High School in the top 10 percent of her class and received the Colonel Sanders KFC Scholarship in 2008.

"My confidence was a little shot when I applied for the KFC scholarship," Gordon admitted. "I applied for other smaller scholarships, and even though my grades were high, I didn't get them. When I found out I won the KFC Scholarship, I was like, 'Oh my gosh!' It was such a large amount—$20,000—and the pool of applicants was so big. I remember thinking, 'It's like when you go buy a lottery ticket—what are the odds?' I'm glad I just said, 'What the hey' and put my heart into the KFC application."

When the day arrived for Anreka's scholarship award ceremony, three cars pulled up in the parking lot of my Poughkeepsie

KFC store, and about 20 people piled out to attend her dinner. She was so excited and had invited her family and some friends too.

"It was a BIG DEAL for me," Gordon recalled. "Mrs. Pfeiffer said, 'Whoa, you've got a big family!' and was so polite and welcoming. I was thrilled to meet this person who was so generous. My mom raised me as a single parent, and we were a low-income, immigrant family. My mom was working herself to the bone, and we didn't know where the money to send me to college would come from. Mrs. Pfeiffer was so joyful and excited and has been open arms with me ever since that first meeting."

Gordon attended Dutchess Community College (now SUNY Dutchess) and graduated in 2010 on the Dean's List. She got a presidential scholarship for her first two years at the community college and earned an associate's degree in business administration. Though her counterparts applied to dozens of four-year schools, she had her mind set on just one.

"For the first time in my life, I actually shed tears of joy when I saw the big green envelope from SUNY Binghamton, and I'm not a real emotional person. All I could think was 'I'm really going away to a four-year school and I'm the first one in my family to do this. This is really happening!'" said Gordon. "I called Mrs. Pfeiffer to let her know I got in."

While Anreka attended community college, the two of us got together for an occasional lunch. Gordon said, "Mrs. Pfeiffer played a large role in my life—not only with the generous scholarship to help me go to college, but also as a mentor to a young woman. When you're from a lower-income family, you don't circulate in the same places as people from the upper and middle class. You don't rub shoulders with CEOs and department managers, so you don't develop the communication, social skills and confidence in those spaces."

The young woman had been disappointed by her participation in a middle school mentorship program at age 14, which paired her with an executive from a local corporation. "I met with her once or twice," Gordon recalled. "I didn't know how to engage in a mentoring relationship with a professional. I was expecting her to teach me, but it didn't seem like she was trying. She wasn't as enthusiastic as I was, so I got discouraged from that experience.

"Mrs. Pfeiffer was the first businessperson I was in really close contact with," Gordon continued. "When she invited me out for lunch, it was the first time an adult who was not in my family asked me. I was eighteen. It felt super official. I had some of my own money, but worried about how expensive the restaurant might be—I didn't intend to take any more money from her! She was so intentional, so curious about my life. I noticed as a young person—before I stepped out into the work world—that showing people you care is important. She went above and beyond to get to know me, wanted to be a light in my life. She helped me build confidence around adults and develop the ability to communicate with people from other walks of life," said Gordon of their lunch dates. "Even though she's so busy, if you tell her something and meet again a month or two later, she remembers. Mrs. Pfeiffer's gift of remembering details about people has been a huge factor in her success.

"Thanks to Mrs. Pfeiffer, I didn't have to take out any loans to earn my two degrees. I graduated from SUNY Binghamton with my bachelor's degree in business in 2012," said Gordon, "and completed my master's degree in public administration at Binghamton by 2014. While I was an undergraduate, my mom saved money to pay for my master's degree and when I started grad school, I received a graduate assistantship to pay for my living expenses. I graduated debt-free with two degrees. That was a huge blessing.

"Mrs. Pfeiffer also sent me KFC gift cards while I was in school, which was sweet, nice and always fun to get," she continued. "And then, when I started my first job just after graduating with my master's degree, she blessed me with another monetary gift that was extremely timely. I didn't know that when you start a professional job, there's a lag before getting paid. I had an apartment and bills to pay and though I never told Mrs. Pfeiffer my situation, her gift was the exact amount to cover my needs. It's a joy knowing her, and I'm very thankful we've been able to stay in touch."

After graduation, Gordon worked at SUNY Binghamton in various administrative offices until 2018, staying in touch all the while. "Mrs. Pfeiffer has really taken me under her wing," Gordon continued. "She is so giving, and it's purely from the heart and her desire to give. She says, 'God can use you as an instrument to sow in the lives of others' and she continues to walk that out. Anything she touches is going to be blessed."

In April 2019, at age 29, Gordon moved to Atlanta to begin working in finance as a tax professional. "I remembered how much I love numbers and math," she said. "One of the reasons people are wealthy is because they understand taxes, and they have tax experts on their side. I enjoy helping others to benefit from my knowledge of the tax codes and laws."

Whenever Anreka visits the Hudson Valley, we reconnect. I invite her to my gatherings and we exchange Christmas greetings each year. I always welcome news from her. It's uplifting to be reminded of the positive effect you can have on another's life. Here we are together at the 2017 Gala celebrating my 50th year as KFC owner/franchisee.

DARLENE L. PFEIFFER

Paul DeLisio's Perspective

Wally passed away in January 2002, and my wife, Gloria, had passed too, and Darlene and I began to spend more time together. As always, we enjoyed each other's company as business friends and colleagues, but things took a turn when she invited me to a party she held in Florida for her 65th birthday. I was dating a woman I knew from high school who lived in Boulder, Colorado, and we sat at a table with Darlene's cousin Sue.

We had a delightful time, hearing stories of their childhood together and later Darlene told me Sue commented, "Paul is a nice guy, but there's one thing wrong with him. He's with the wrong woman. He should be with you."

Darlene and I had never really paid attention to each other in that way before but as Darlene said, "When you change the way you look at someone, you change the way they look." Sometimes, somebody else has to point these things out to you, which was fortunate for me.

She and her family like to take cruises, and Darlene likes to dance and was great at it. How many men say, "I don't like to dance," and their wives say, "You just stepped on my feet!" But Darlene says, "You did great! You'll be a great dancer," and it's amazing, getting that encouragement from her and learning to go with the music. People now tell us we're such a beautiful couple on the dance floor. We've had the greatest of times, been in wonderful places together—including the "Dancing With the Stars" fundraiser for the United Way—and many other events where she was recognized for her good works.

Those KFC years were incredible, especially for me, because I tagged along with Darlene for many of her national meetings. There were two, maybe three, meetings each year, and they were always in great places—like the Napa Valley of California and New Orleans. I believe the KFC franchisee system was the greatest business model. Franchisees owned independent businesses bound together by high standards designed to improve their bottom line. There were about 500 other owners who shared a buying co-op, were interested in business efficiency, and they shared a tremendous work ethic that worked for everybody.

At the 2004 KFC convention, I witnessed Darlene raising a million dollars from people who were all her friends, people who really cared about her and about each other. The good will and joy amongst those franchisees at their meetings were wonderful. And back home, she and her employees were frying chicken and cleaning shortening off the floor, yet she created such a great camaraderie in her stores too.

One of her great qualities is her ability to approach a problem as "Let's solve this and let's move on." The number one thing I admire about her is how one person can make such an incredible difference in the lives of so many others. It doesn't matter how many stories you hear about people of great accomplishment: I'm right up close to somebody who has done so many things and who the heck is she? She has a condo in Port Ewen and ran a few KFC stores and she went up against guys who flew on private jets, owned 250 stores and a cattle ranch and they said, "Why don't I just step aside and let Darlene Pfeiffer run this?"

Colonel Sanders once told her you can do things the hard way or you can do things the easy way. If things are easy when you start, as you get to the end, it will be hard. But if you do things the hard way, in the long run, it will be the easy way. That's exactly how she's lived her life: The hard way is the correct way.

She loves to read about U.S. presidents and how they often had to make decisions the majority of the country would not agree with: Congress didn't like it, their own party didn't like it, millions of citizens didn't like it. When she was leading the lawsuit against PepsiCo on behalf of the KFC franchisees, PepsiCo went around her to some franchisees and said, "Why don't you just tell your leaders to go along? Darlene is on an ego trip." But it didn't work because the majority of the

DARLENE L. PFEIFFER

franchisees understood they were all in the fight together. Darlene was one of very few women in positions of power at that time, and she used it for the greater good. And it wasn't like she just stood up and split the mountain open with one movement of her arm. She kept moving with great focus and energy and many good things happened as a result.

Darlene has never operated on what others thought of her but has always been job-focused and able to accomplish things with a bit of glamor or natural flare. There is no one who can get dressed faster than Darlene. She can go from being in her nightie to looking like a million bucks in five minutes. I'm chugging along, putting things in my pockets and looking for my jacket, and she's standing by the door, ready to go, looking glamorous. She says her ability to get ready to go so fast started when she was a flight attendant, worried she'd miss the bus to the airport. Every time we go out, people tell her "I love your shoes" or ask her if she's a movie star. It's because of the way she carries and conducts herself. People know she's something special, and that giving heart of hers shines through.

Paul DeLisio & Darlene Dancing with the Stars Ulster Style, 2015.

CHAPTER 25

Mentoring is Giving

To be successful in business, everyone needs to develop a team. Effective leaders create an atmosphere conducive to growth and increased responsibility, and one of the most valuable things employees can do to build their skillsets is to shadow a leader. Mentoring to encourage people to stretch in new directions is among the most gratifying aspects of running your own business.

The only thing I miss from the days when I ran my restaurants is the people, and thankfully two of my former Kentucky Fried Chicken employees—Joe Farley and Christine Fautz—are still in my life on a daily basis. Each of them exemplifies my philosophy about people development and the importance of creating a team. No one can do it all, and you can't achieve your goals unless you surround yourself with the right people.

Joe came to work for me when he was 17—his first day was September 9, 1993, which was also Colonel Sanders' birthday—and was hired as a front-counter customer service worker at my South Road KFC store in Poughkeepsie. A bright young man, he progressed quickly to cook, assistant manager, and then he became manager of two of my stores—one in Kingston and the one in Poughkeepsie—at age 19. Joe eventually became my director of operations and, in 2009, an equity partner: He ran those two stores until I sold them in 2019. Joe recently invested in a condominium in a recreational community in Pennsylvania and called me 10 minutes after he closed the deal. We talk every day and I love him like a son.

When Joe came onboard, I was busy flying around the country to fulfill my regional and national duties on behalf of the KFC franchisees. The previous manager trained him and he attracted my notice for his strong work ethic.

Every one of my employees started in entry-level positions. All of them came to me as high school students or graduates, and none were college grads. I believe in treating every employee with respect and love: There's nothing I wouldn't do for my employees, and them for me. As my right-hand man, Joe followed my lead of working together as partners. We shared an office and talked every day, even when I wasn't onsite. He always developed a key person who worked under him, furthering the model he learned from me.

Joe Farley's Perspective

"I owe everything I've done in my life to Mrs. Pfeiffer," said Joe. "Each day we would discuss sales, operations, mystery shops, how to develop our teams and have a bench plan. One of the things I learned from her was you never know what's going to happen—which is exciting, but also means there will be a problem every day and you need to be prepared for all kinds of things."

Joe admitted he used to get excited and react. "I'd say, 'Oh my god, what are we going to do about that?' but she was always calm, and I asked her how she did it. She said, 'I've been through it all and it taught me to become a great problem solver and to believe I'll get through it. If you're excited, angry, stressed, it's difficult to see problems clearly or to solve them. It works better if you stay calm'."

For Joe, there were many occasions to put her advice to work, but one stands out. "Mrs. Pfeiffer and I had just flown to Florida for the KFC national convention in 2007 when the Kingston store manager called to tell me the store was on fire and asked what he should do. I told him to pull the Ansul System [a fire suppression system that releases wet chemical extinguishing agents to protect the hoods, appliances and plenum areas with a wet chemical that can't re-ignite], and watch it burn."

He explained: "When I told Mrs. Pfeiffer the Kingston store was on fire and flames were coming through the roof, she said, 'Is the fire department there and are they working on putting it out?' When I said yes, she said, 'OK, let's go to the bar and have a couple of drinks and discuss it.' It was obviously a big problem and a stressful situation, but in the end, we came out much better. The store was rebuilt and eventually in good shape, and she stayed calm throughout it all."

Another thing Joe learned was how to encounter adversity and plan ahead. "Now, I have a conversation with myself first to anticipate what others might say and to know what I want to get out of any situation," said Joe. "I teach my managers to not have conversations when they are aggravated, but rather to go home, take a breath, and think about what they want to accomplish before having a discussion. I learned that from Mrs. Pfeiffer and there's not much that surprises me as a result."

Though Joe was outgoing towards our customers at the stores, I kept pushing him to get onto the national KFC boards like I did. Public speaking was not in his comfort zone, but he eventually ran meetings for hundreds of people.

"I became the KFC Northeast Regional AKFCF president in her honor," said Joe. "I wanted to do it for her and would never have done it without her encouragement. All the things we've done for schools and helping people in the community—like coming up with the idea for the KFC Northeast Gold Tournament and raising forty thousand dollars for scholarships—wouldn't have happened. Whenever they honor Mrs. Pfeiffer at ceremonies at SUNY Ulster, I always attend. At one of them, she had me stand up and said, 'As long as Joe keeps bringing in the money at the stores, I can keep donating'," he said.

"She definitely was my mentor and we became great friends after that. I help her with anything I can," Joe continued. "The funny thing is, there's no 'Hey, I can't do that' with her. It's 'Let's figure this out' instead. To this day, no matter what I'm doing, like remodeling a house or anything at all, when I encounter a problem, I think about how I can fix it. I feel there's no problem I cannot overcome. When I was running her stores and looking after more than sixty employees, I was young and her influence was huge. She taught me a lot. You couldn't get much better than her."

But Pfeiffer extends the same compliment to him. "Joe is definitely a can-do kind of person," she said. "If I ask him, 'Can you fix X, Y or Z, he'll say, CERTAINLY!' It's his favorite word. He never says, 'I think I can' or 'I'll have to call somebody about that.' He just says, 'Certainly!' whether it's about something for me, for himself or anyone else."

Joe attended several national KFC conventions and noted, "There were billboards with all the names of the past presidents, and her name was there twice—nobody else was there twice. And the craziness that happened when she walked into the room! Everyone missed her, wanted to say hi, and one of the coolest things was she knew the names of everyone in people's families, their dog's name, events they shared together. When she walked into the exhibition hall, she got stopped every second," he said. "I was twenty or twenty-one when I first attended and had no idea what she meant to KFC. As the years went by, I would just go do my work because I couldn't get anywhere when I walked in with her. All of the vendors and franchisees have a personal history together and back then, she was in the midst of doing it all."

Of having moved up from being a cashier at one KFC store to becoming a franchisee of record who served as president of the KFC Northeast Regional AKFCF, Joe said simply, "She transformed my career, starting from working just a few hours a week while I was in high school. The best training is on-the-job and learning as it comes, and there's nothing better than doing that every day. She definitely did not let me stay in my comfort zone, and I did things I thought I would never ever do."

During his tenure as president of the KFC Northeast Regional AKFCF, Joe received an award at a ceremony recognizing his efforts to raise funding for student scholarships. "It was a bronze statue of me as a golfer with a caddy," he said. "Nobody can do it on their own, the caddy is there to help, and I brought her up and recognized her."

"And one more thing: In all the time I've known her, I have never seen her raise her voice. When I get angry, words sometimes come out that shouldn't," Joe said. "Mrs. Pfeiffer might be aggravated, but she always speaks in the same tone. She knows everything will be fine."

Like Joe, Chris Fautz started working at my store when she was 17. A friend whose mother was a big fan of KFC suggested Chris apply for a job. She was ready for her senior year of high school and my son-in-law, Walter, hired her in 1984 to work at the front counter. Chris became store manager in 1987 and worked in that position for two years until she took a maternity leave. She returned to work as a shift manager, then got pregnant with her second child and later worked her way up to an office position, where she helped with mailings, payroll and other clerical duties. In 1999, Chris and her husband had their third child and when she returned to work for me in January 2002, she took care of bookkeeping, accounting, ordering and other necessities so I could stay on top of my store operations.

Chris Fautz's Perspective

"The first time I met Mrs. Pfeiffer," Chris recalled, "I had been working at the store for a while and someone said, 'Mrs. Pfeiffer is coming!' and everyone scurried around to be on their best behavior. But she was young, beautiful and vibrant, and she remembered all the little things about all of us—saying 'Your son was sick, how is he now?'—and I was very shocked. She was so, so nice, and my impression of her hasn't changed much since then."

Chris said their relationship has grown over the years but is not formal. "I consider Mrs. Pfeiffer to be a part of my family.

My kids love her, my husband thinks of her as a second mother, and she, Joe and I call ourselves 'the Three Amigos' because there isn't anything we can't do together. She's been a boss, mentor, friend, but she's family first and everything falls behind that. I don't technically work for her in a professional capacity now, but I do help her out one day a week."

"I have learned so much from her—how to problem solve, how important it is to be punctual and not waste people's time—but mostly how to be positive. It's not always easy when you're facing a challenge, but as she says, 'Look at the bright side, just flip it,' which helped me learn to ask myself 'Can I fix it, can I do something about it?' I'm able to look at things objectively. Sometimes things are just bad, and you have to ride them out; other times, you can be proactive and try to fix the situation."

A few years ago, Chris submitted an application to nominate Darlene Pfeiffer as her Raising Hope mentor. "They are a part of the United Way and Mrs. Pfeiffer was chosen as one of the mentors. It was one of her hundreds of awards, but that one was from me," said Chris.

Said Pfeiffer: "When we were at the awards ceremony, another woman who nominated a mentor got up to speak and talked for 15 minutes. Chris looked over at me, and I knew she hadn't prepared a lengthy speech. True to her succinct nature, she walked to the podium, introduced me and said, 'Mrs. Pfeiffer is a great person to work for,' which was direct and to the point, just like she is. I felt tremendously proud and touched by her nomination."

For Chris, the feeling is mutual. "Mrs. Pfeiffer is a very giving person," she said. "When Mrs. Fleming gave her a scholarship to go to college, it really stuck with her, and she helped all three of my kids go to college. My youngest daughter still has lunch with her from time to time. Mrs. Pfeiffer has long relationships with people because she puts herself out there, keeps in touch and is interested in what you have to say."

DREAM BIG, ADD MOXIE

> Pfeiffer's style is "quiet and firm, sometimes very firm, but she doesn't yell or get angry," Chris added, echoing Joe's impression of her leadership style. "If she says, 'Help me to understand this,' you need to follow because it is not good. She's very even-keeled and even though I've seen things go bad over the years, she is always calm, collected and specific.
>
> "She's very frugal too. She will take you out to dinner, but she's part of a generation that knew how to make things last," Chris continued. "She had a forty-year-old coffee percolator we had to replace, and that was something."
>
> Pfeiffer agreed. "Chris is right," she said. "When I look at items, I say to myself, 'Do I need this, or do I want it?' To this day, if I don't need it, I walk away. I only buy something if I need it, which is an important lesson to learn."

Small and large life lessons can add up to big life differences. I keep that in mind when mentoring young people who may not have a lot of work or life experience when we first meet. Though I may take good habits and organizational skills for granted now, these daily practices are new to them and need to be nurtured. The way you live your life can be a strong, positive example for others and when you're blessed to be around good people, you may reap the added benefit of forming strong bonds that last for decades.

(L to R): Darlene, Candace Carr, Paul Scism, Joe Farley, Kristi Farley and Christine Fautz celebrate the holidays in 2005.

CLOCKWISE FROM ABOVE

SUNY Ulster President Dr. Alan P. Roberts with the late Foundation Board Chair, Anita WIlliams Peck and Foundation Vice Chair and Donor, Darlene Pfeiffer.

Darlene and Dr. Ann Marrott, Vice President Emerita & Foundation Director Emerita.

Darlene and Carlos Cuellar, SUNY Ulster student scholarship recipient of the Daniel Perez Cueva Scholarship for Immigrants by Darlene L. Pfeiffer.

Dr. Mindy Kole greets Darlene at the SUNY Ulster Ownit! Entrepreneurial Women's Conference.

FACING PAGE

Top – Darlene at the Opening and Ribbon Cutting for the SUNY Ulster Pfeiffer Technology & Innovation Lab.

Bottom – Lorraine Salmon, executive director, Ulster Community College Foundation with Darlene and Dr. Ann Marrott.

PART FOUR

SUNY Ulster
Giving Fearlessly

Top – October 19, 2017, Pfeiffer Technology & Innovation Lab Opening.
Bottom – Paul DeLisio and Darlene.

CHAPTER 26

Focus on the Impact

There were many times in my life when I learned the ropes from more experienced business owners, and now I wanted to help lay the groundwork for others. I understand the personal dedication and financial resources needed to obtain a college education.

My college education formed an important foundation to achieve my goals—first as a flight attendant for TWA and later as a successful businesswoman in the male-dominated fast-food industry. As a high school graduate, I received two scholarships established by Mrs. Bruck Fleming in her son Philip's name, which helped fund my freshman and sophomore years at Capital University in Columbus, Ohio. I finally earned my bachelor's degree when I returned to college in my late 30s. My then-husband, Jan, was not enthusiastic about my return to college—he wanted me to be 'a good wife' and didn't want me involved in my KFC businesses either—so my determination to obtain my college degree became a watershed moment for me.

By the time our divorce was finalized in January 1977, I had earned my bachelor's degree in political science from SUNY New Paltz with summa cum laude honors. However, our divorce settlement left me with just three of my nine stores and $140,000 of debt Jan incurred while he nearly bankrupted my KFC stores. Bevy had come to live with me a few years earlier when her mother died of cancer, so I was a single mother as well.

I carried my commitment to college scholarship programs with me into my expanding responsibilities at Kentucky Fried Chicken—and helped establish, and then dramatically grow, their impact throughout the United States. Five Ulster County students were direct recipients of these $20,000 KFC scholarships, but I wanted to have a greater impact on the lives of local students.

Mrs. Fleming, who awarded me two scholarships to support my college education, first revealed the compounding effect of generosity and giving to me when I had just finished high school, but I was too young then to fully grasp the message. However, my brief visits with her left a deep impression on me. Today, I carry that forward by requiring scholarship recipients at SUNY Ulster to meet with me in-person once a semester. This is sometimes an opportunity for an occasional bit of mentoring and, more importantly, lets me hear their goals and make it clear to them I value their efforts to get an education and make positive changes in their lives.

In 2004, when I spearheaded an expansion of the Colonel Sanders Kentucky Fried Chicken Scholarship Program for graduating high school seniors nationwide, I was increasingly concerned about the brain drain out of Ulster County. I wanted to encourage young people to stay here to start their own businesses following graduation.

Ulster County was still trying to recover from the ripple effect of IBM closing its facilities in Kingston. Beginning in 1956 and lasting four decades, the IBM facilities in Dutchess, Westchester and Ulster counties were a primary source of employment and economic development for the region. At its peak in 1985, the IBM site in the Town of Ulster on the outskirts of Kingston, New York, employed up to 7,100 workers in its manufacturing plant and engineering laboratory. Its boom years profoundly impacted IBM employees and their families, and spawned the growth of small businesses, expansion in numerous civic and educational institutions, and the creation of housing developments in suburban neighborhoods throughout the Kingston area. When IBM announced in 1994 it would be closing its Kingston plant, the reverberations were widespread: Decades later, the local rise and fall of IBM is cited as a major factor in the continuing transformation of Ulster County.

After IBM departed the area, many students and professionals moved out of the region in droves because of the dramatic downturn in employment. I thought, "We've got to get work in Ulster County. Otherwise, this is going to turn into a death town."

> **Bevy Hung's Perspective: Part 4**
>
> The way my mother, Darlene, thinks about philanthropy earned my respect. Ordinary people who aren't millionaires 10 times over do not normally give at her level, but she believes we all should be able to give something—maybe not as much as those who are very rich, but we can all do something. Darlene's path from flight attendant to being a successful businesswoman didn't happen overnight though it did happen quickly, because that's the kind of person she is. She always has a focus, always strives to be productive, and is even more goal-oriented in her later years. It was like a scene out of *Beaches* when Darlene got me. She had her franchise restaurants, was an older woman who had gone back to college in her 30s—nobody did that back then—and had a sense of herself, what she wanted to do, and she went for it.
>
> The beauty, the wonder, of my mother is her innate ability to always be evolving. She is not a stagnant person and looks for ways to improve herself and her environment. She had the foresight to go into a career she loved and to travel, and then moved on to the world of business. Franchises were just starting back then, and she was definitely ahead of her time when she began her Kentucky Fried Chicken stores.
>
> Her focus on "enjoy giving while you're here" was also ahead of the curve, very forward-thinking. When Darlene started giving to SUNY Ulster several years ago, her approach and her goals were grounded in that philosophy.

CHAPTER 27

Darlene L. Pfeiffer Scholarships

I became aware of Ulster County Community College (now known as SUNY Ulster, part of the State University of New York system) when a class president who loved KFC hired me to provide a buffet for his graduating class picnic. Ward Todd is a well-known Ulster County personality—first as a popular radio talk show host and former chair of the Ulster County Legislature, and more recently as the long-time president of the Ulster County Regional Chamber of Commerce—and he was the first person to put this educational gem on my radar. But few people are aware of his distinction as my first KFC catering client!

Around this time, I decided to devote my attention to help SUNY Ulster students in need—and that's when I met Marianne Collins, former director of the SUNY Ulster Foundation.

"Darlene picked up the phone, called the college and asked for a meeting," recalled Collins. "One thing everybody knows about Darlene is that when she decides to act, she means NOW!"

Since then, said Collins, "Darlene has had a very strong predisposition to assisting students, especially women students, and even more so, students who seemed to need an extra little push, a voice of support and recognition, someone who was on their side. Her life and business experience brought her into contact with entry-level, lower-wage workers, and she had empathy for their concerns. Together, these experiences solidified her desire to share herself and her resources with others."

Collins noted I was drawn to those students due to my

own experiences. "Darlene gravitated to those students, in large part because of how much the scholarship she received had meant in her life. She had the opportunity—rare in those days—to meet her scholarship donor," Collins pointed out, "and connected her own good fortune with another person's desire to do good. Now, she was ready to follow through with action."

In 2005, I contributed my first $5,000 scholarship gift for students—and this support continues at ten $1,000 scholarships per year today—but I wanted to do more to prepare students to become entrepreneurs.

While there were some fine points and details to work out, I arrived at my initial meetings with SUNY Ulster representatives knowing what I wanted to do: I wanted my contributions to be more targeted to business and entrepreneurship in light of the economic downturn Ulster County was still experiencing following IBM's departure from Kingston. I wanted to help women with financial needs, and especially those with additional barriers or challenges to completing their education. And I wanted to be directly involved in selecting the scholars who would receive assistance.

"This direct involvement is sometimes a difficult proposition," said Collins, "but not with Darlene. She understood and easily complied with an arms-length approach. Most important to her was she wanted the opportunity to meet, and possibly come to know, these women and perhaps mentor them if appropriate. Her excellent judgement led her to make clear she was invested in these women if they wanted her to be. She was never intrusive but let them know she would be in their corner."

Collins added, "It was the most unique scholarship program we stewarded. And, as much as Darlene wanted to assist and mentor students, she keenly spotted other ways to help the college achieve some of its goals more fully."

One of the first things I did was put together the Start Here Go Far Boutique of gently used, excellent quality clothing of all types for students to supplement or be the basis of their wardrobe. I knew many students didn't have the proper attire to attend professional-level functions or make a good impression at job interviews, and I started by cleaning out my own closet and asking others for donations. The boutique opened in 2011 and some of the clothes received were so attractive that faculty and staff also browsed there from time to time. Students and their families were able to replace a lot of clothing lost in Superstorm Sandy from the stock in the boutique.

When I joined the Ulster Community College Foundation board of directors in 2010, it was essentially composed of men, as was true for most boards at that time. I came on ready to offer financial support as well as the benefit of my experience in business.

Lorraine Salmon, the current executive director the Ulster Community College Foundation, said that I was "not just one of the first women to serve on our board: she arrived while giving. Back in 1980, our foundation fundraising efforts brought in $75,000 in one year. In 2021, our Foundation manages $14-15 million in assets and Darlene was a large part of the change that occurred during these years."

Salmon continued: "When Darlene and (the late) Anita Peck were both serving on the board of directors, their individual giving was even greater than that of our largest corporate sponsors. Darlene and Anita evolved into super-givers. According to a July 2018 article in *Forbes* magazine, most of the private wealth that will change hands in the coming decades is likely to go to women. In the coming decades, we anticipate our foundation board will be continually strengthened by powerful senior women, like the two of them, who are staking a claim on the world of philanthropy."

An article published in *The Economist* published on International Women's Day in 2018—entitled "Investment by women, and in them, is growing"—boldly stated that between 2010 and 2015, private wealth held by women grew from $34 trillion to $51 trillion, an increase of 50 percent in merely five years. Moreover, most of the private wealth that will change hands in the coming decades is likely to go to women.

Salmon said I helped reshape her thinking about what an individual is capable of doing as a giver. "At an earlier point in my life while I was raising two children on my own, I had been giving St. Jude's Hospital fifty dollars per month, which didn't feel like enough," Salmon admitted. "I wasn't sure I was making a difference. Then I calculated this monthly gift, restating it at six hundred dollars per year, and that felt better to me. When I began to annualize my giving, it made me see a bigger possibility and it changed my outlook on contributions and their impact. Today, giving is part of my personal drive."

"When I met Darlene much later in life when my children were grown, out of college and having families of their own," Salmon continued, "I realized Darlene was always reminding people it's not about a dollar amount but rather about giving and being part of a larger giving community. That is what giving turned out to be for me—being part of a community of people helping others. And I learned again, watching Darlene, it adds up over time, over a year, over a lifetime."

Darlene with Ulster Community College Foundation, Inc. Executive Director Lorraine Salmon and Dr. Mindy Kole, Director of the Pfeiffer Center for Entrepreneurial Studies.

CHAPTER 28

Darlene L. Pfeiffer Scholarship Recipient Profile: Jill Costello

Jill Costello received the Darlene L. Pfeiffer Scholarship from SUNY Ulster and graduated with an Associate in Science degree in Nursing at SUNY Ulster in 2008. The program is accredited by the Accreditation Commission for Education in Nursing (ACEN) and graduates are eligible to take the National Council Licensure Examination for Registered Nurses (NCLEX-RN).

At age 34, Costello had been a stay-at-home mom for 11 years until she caught her husband cheating and went home to stay at her parents' house with her four kids, then aged nine, seven, four and two. Her grandmother was bed-bound under hospice care while dying of breast cancer which had metastasized to her brain; the family gathered around to take care of her. "I had the most time, so I took care of her most often," Costello recalled. "Gram always called me her favorite nurse, and I would say, 'It's me, Gram. I'm not a nurse.' The last thing she said to me before she died was, 'Just remember, you're my favorite nurse.' I replied, 'I'm not a nurse,' and she said, 'Well, you should be'."

Costello's car had been re-possessed (her father bought her another one). Her mother had given her a security deposit for an apartment. She had no money and faced having to take out loans to go to school, but everything fell into place when she decided to apply for scholarships to enroll in the nursing program at SUNY Ulster.

She received some of the scholarships, including the Darlene L. Pfeiffer Scholarship for $1,000. "Her only stipulation was you had to be a single mom, and you had to tell her why you were returning to college and how you were doing," said Costello. "If you were chosen, you had to have lunch with her at the college in the conference room. The first day we met, she brought Kentucky Fried Chicken for our lunch and we hit it off. She said she'd told the financial aid office she wanted to give me $1,000 every semester for four semesters: The only thing she asked was for the two of us to have lunch at the beginning of every semester so I could tell her my plan for the year, how my grades were, and how my kids were doing."

"We never met outside of those meetings, and didn't form a lasting friendship, but she wanted to know I was still in school. I was not high risk—I come from an extremely large, supportive, successful family—but I wasn't going to ask my parents for money. I funded my education all by myself, and she literally paid for half of my associate degree."

Costello calls nursing her third career. She first worked in fashion and retail after attending Fashion Institute of Technology in Manhattan and held jobs at Calvin Klein, Ann Taylor and Macy's until she had her third child and realized traveling back and forth from Orange County to New York City was too much. Her second career, full-time motherhood, was quite demanding—with four kids she was busy with the PTA, soccer club and homemaking—but after her divorce and her grandmother's death, Costello wanted to live on her own with her children. She moved to Ulster County, where she met the man who would become her second husband and began her nursing studies at SUNY Ulster.

"I held down two or three jobs during nursing school and lived in a one-bedroom apartment with my four kids," she said. "All five of us did our homework together at the dining room table. It was one of our closest times and I wouldn't trade it for the world but yes, it was extremely hard. My second husband was a lifesaver: He 'babysat' my kids while I was working and going to school."

Following graduation, Costello passed the licensing exam and received her RN license from the New York State Board for Professional Licensure. Today, she is a registered nurse and an instructor for the American Heart Association, for Critical Care and Trauma Care, where she certifies/recertifies medical professionals in basic and advanced lifesaving.

In the course of her two-year degree program and after getting her RN license, Costello worked as an emergency room nurse and a phlebotomist and had a year-long residency at Westchester Medical Center in the cardio-thoracic unit. She tried hospice and oncology too, but always went back to the ER.

Today, she and her husband enjoy dual residencies in Ulster County and Florida. She works per diem at four different medical facilities, logging between 10 and 70 hours a week. At 52 years old, she has two grandchildren and one more on the way.

"I hadn't seen Darlene Pfeiffer except at my daughter's SUNY Ulster graduation ceremony. I re-introduced myself to her, but we didn't keep in touch after that," said Costello. Then, in 2021, she was working one of her per diem jobs at a surgical center in Dutchess County when she saw Pfeiffer's name on the list for a surgical procedure and asked to be assigned to take care of her.

"Before she went into surgery, I said, 'You're Darlene Pfeiffer from Ulster County, aren't you?' She replied, 'Yes. Do we know each other?' Standing over her, I got tears in my eyes when I said, 'We do. You paid for a huge portion of my nursing school. You're why I'm working as a nurse today.' Back in 2008, Darlene was really busy, so she remembered me but not the details. I'm glad I had the opportunity to talk to her and tell her how fortunate I feel to be one of the students she helped. I never thought I'd be divorced, and I never thought I'd be a nurse either, but her scholarship support was one of the interventions that led me to my path. I wanted so desperately to do nursing school on my own and Darlene, as a woman, understood in a way not everyone can."

CHAPTER 29

The Darlene L. Pfeiffer Center for Entrepreneurial Studies

I set a goal to start an entrepreneurial center on the SUNY Ulster campus because I wanted to do something to encourage community college graduates to create and find meaningful work here in Ulster County. The first thing I did was to have a conversation with Dr. Donald Katt, the president of SUNY Ulster from 2001-2015, to discuss my idea: He liked it and we continued to talk about how to get the ball rolling. I was ready to make a $100,000 contribution and met with Marianne Collins and Dr. Anita Bleffert-Schmidt, then chair of the Business Department.

Collins recalled how the project developed: "When Darlene teamed up with Dr. Mindy Kole, then a part-time adjunct faculty member of the Business and Professional Studies Department at SUNY Ulster, all of their shared interests really took shape," she said. "The college was just introducing a concentration in Entrepreneurial Studies and Kole—who had great vision, energy and enthusiasm—was leading it. When Darlene and Mindy met, you could practically see the electricity in the room. Mindy had begun to offer afternoon seminars by regional business leaders and invited Darlene to be one of the presenters. She proved to be a natural—inspirational, practical and funny. Darlene's accessible and approachable nature attracted students and her session became a highlight of the series."

Around that time, I attended a breakfast meeting of the Ulster County Chamber of Commerce where Dr. Nancy Zimpher, who became the 12th chancellor of the State University of New York in 2009, was the speaker. It turned out she was also from Ohio, and we had a very nice chat. Although we had already put some wheels in motion, I said to Dr. Zimpher, "Based on your great talk, I've come up with the idea of having an Entrepreneurial Center on the SUNY Ulster campus." She and I became rather close, and this is a good example of how giving another person credit for an idea is one way to draw them in.

As the driving force behind the new Entrepreneurial Women's Conference (OWN It!) at SUNY Ulster, Mindy Kole was a magnet who attracted other people's enthusiasm. With my encouragement and advocacy, the conference became a well-supported annual event that enhanced the reputation of both the Business Department and SUNY Ulster as a whole.

When I was invited to join the SUNY Ulster Foundation's board of directors, Collins noted that I "quickly became an important voice, adding a sense of vision and possibility, as well as keen analytical questioning to the meetings." During that period, I continued to expand my financial support to the college with special attention to the Business Department and its impact on the lives of women receiving help through the scholarships I had already established.

"Darlene envisioned the Business & Professional Studies Department giving these women the skills and self-assurance to succeed financially," said Collins. "We had many conversations about this, and Darlene was convinced the way to achieve these goals was for Professor Kole to become full-time and lead the efforts on behalf of the department. She believed this investment would improve enrollments in the business programs."

Thanks to "the marvelous mutual admiration that Mindy and Darlene felt about each other and Darlene's absolute determination to see Mindy join the full-time faculty so her energy and scholarship would have greater reach," said Collins, "Darlene was like a steam train and she was definitely on the right track as history has proven."

And Kole joined that steam train right away. "I didn't

know what to expect but I loved Darlene from the beginning," she said. "She's so kindly and graciously endowed our Center for Entrepreneurial Studies and was respectful of our ideas about what it would be. She always has wonderful ideas for me, and our vision became a wonderful partnership really quickly."

Because of my background in sales and marketing, I understood the value of creating a welcoming place for students and faculty to gather, build relationships and create a business student's identity. "So, Darlene also underwrote the costs associated with redesigning the Business & Professional Studies office space," said Collins. "And, at the request of the college, she agreed to be recognized for her contributions—financial, personal commitment of vision, encouragement and boots on the ground engagement. Darlene's name was placed on the newly renovated offices and conference room."

The 2011 ribbon-cutting ceremony for the Darlene L. Pfeiffer Center for Entrepreneurial Studies was attended by the highly regarded SUNY Chancellor, Dr. Nancy Zimpher, as well as elected officials, local dignitaries and business leaders. "There is nothing like a visit from the SUNY Chancellor to rivet attention on a college and put fear into the hearts of the administration. Not surprisingly, Darlene charmed Chancellor Zimpher, and they began a robust correspondence," Collins recalled. "In fact, in one of Dr. Zimpher's hallmark programs, Darlene joined the Chancellor and several other significant SUNY philanthropists at a reception in New York City to be recognized for their outstanding contributions to public higher education in New York State."

Today, the Center is housed in SUNY Ulster's Business & Professional Studies Department and its Entrepreneurial Studies Certificate program is targeted at students who want to own their own business. With its emphasis on technology and sustainability, the center works closely with the Department of Continuing and Professional Education, the Mid-Hudson Regional Small Business Development Center,

Ulster County Economic Development Alliance and the Ulster County Regional Chamber of Commerce. Collaborative programs for students, faculty, alumni, entrepreneurs, business leaders, mentors and government agencies focus on a wide range of entrepreneurial projects. Offerings include a speaker series, student-run campus business, business plan competition, membership in the National Association for Community College Entrepreneurship (NACCE), and opportunities for students to work with local companies on business needs such as marketing and advertising.

As a faculty member in the Business & Professional Studies Department, Kole teaches entrepreneurship, advanced entrepreneurship, marketing management, business ethics, and is an advisor for the students in the department's degree programs. The Darlene L. Pfeiffer Center for Entrepreneurial Studies enriches students' education with extra activities and also serves the larger community.

"One example," said Kole, "is our SUNY Ulster Women's OWN It! Conference, which ran for five consecutive years until COVID-19 forced us to cancel it in 2020. We will pick it up again when things return to normal as it was very successful and well-attended. We offered a full day of workshops, excellent keynote speakers and action-oriented workshops— no fluff. I wanted to offer concrete, actionable sessions for women entrepreneurs," Kole explained, "and we organized it with three tiers of participation. There are dozens of workshops with a focus on networking and camaraderie, things like how to sell effectively or get financing. OWN It! is held here on our beautiful campus and it takes our team a whole year to work on it."

SUNY Ulster students in the Business & Professional Studies Department benefit from a dedicated team of faculty members and an administration that partners with others to create a range of opportunities for students. One prime example is their collaboration with Marist College to support the Mid-Hudson Business Plan Competition. It feeds into the

DREAM BIG, ADD MOXIE

New York State Business Plan Competition, which has helped launch hundreds of student-led ventures, provided more than a million dollars in prize money, and supported more than $150 million in private investment and economic value. "It offers serious money and we always have students who enter into the competition, which features a variety of speakers and coaches and is aimed at students who want to start a business," said Kole. "Entry into the competition connects them with the Mid-Hudson Business Development Center, housed at SUNY Ulster, which offers a wealth of resources."

"Darlene is really one of a kind," added Collins. "She possesses a truly keen mind, a very kind heart, and a savvy understanding of human and organizational behavior. Collaborating, blue-skying, and implementing together with her were some of the most enjoyable times I spent at SUNY Ulster."

The 2011 ribbon-cutting ceremony for the Darlene L. Pfeiffer Center for Entrepreneurial Studies, attended by SUNY Chancellor, Dr. Nancy Zimpher, as well as elected officials, local dignitaries and business leaders.

CHAPTER 30

The Pfeiffer Technology & Innovation Lab

After Don Katt retired, Dr. Alan Roberts, who is affectionately known as "Dr. Al," became president of SUNY Ulster in 2015 and I was one of the people who served on the search committee to select him for the position. I remember speaking with Dr. Al's closest colleague at his previous position at a community college in southern Florida. He told me when Dr. Al first came to their college as a vice president, people were operating in individual silos. They didn't talk with each other or share ideas. Dr. Al, who played guitar, started a band and invited his new colleagues to come play music with him on Friday afternoons. He told everyone, "I don't care if you can play well, just come. We'll have fun together." All those who participated became friends and began to talk and share ideas within a year. It made all the difference in the world and was a smart way to bring people together.

I called Dr. Al a couple of days after he started working at SUNY Ulster, introduced myself and invited him to dinner at a restaurant on the Hudson River.

Dr. Al remembers our meeting this way: "Darlene's reputation preceded her," he said. "Everyone was talking about what an incredible lady she is, how giving and caring she is, and how she's changing lives. We had a lovely meal by the river, and Darlene told me what her expectations were, including some stories about people who had disappointed her. She gave me my marching orders right off the bat, but she did it in a lovely way. She tells stories that are interesting and motivating," he added. "I always know I can reach out to her with questions and concerns, and she will always be there to help."

The first major initiative Dr. Al and I worked on together was upgrading a technology facility on the campus. Before he arrived at SUNY Ulster, there had been discussions about moving the lab off campus but, like me, he firmly believed it needed to be on campus.

"I believe the future is in technology," said Dr. Al, "but our offerings needed to be state-of-the-art to prepare our students. It wasn't in the cards, though, without more support. Darlene understood and contributed $100,000 as seed money for an eventual $950,000 project. The Pfeiffer Technology & Innovation Lab opened in 2017 and today it's a remarkable center with smart rooms and advanced technologies. It's the largest, most significant technology facility on our Stone Ridge campus."

The lab houses training and testing equipment used by students who are pursuing degrees in STEM disciplines, including engineering, advanced manufacturing, AutoCAD, 3D printing and web development. In keeping with SUNY Ulster's goal of fostering and supporting collaborations between education and the advanced technology and manufacturing industry, this facility helps support the competitive edge of local companies and serves as a resource for the manufacturing industry by providing real-world experience for students.

Three labs and two classrooms were thoroughly renovated and outfitted with the latest equipment. In addition to students studying STEM disciplines, the drafting and 3D printing labs now serve the needs of students in industrial technology, drafting, computer, graphic design, art and fashion. The electronics lab received new electronic benches, and the Mechatronics and Mechanical Engineering Lab is outfitted with new work benches and a private outside entrance for industry partners. Classroom renovations included 18 new computers and training units, both of which use Programmable Logic Controller (PLC) software. A classroom without computers was upgraded to allow students to both learn in a classroom section and then do hands-on experiments in the lab; both are available for any department to use.

Darlene at the grand opening of the Pfeiffer Technology & Innovation Lab at SUNY Ulster, October 19, 2017.

CHAPTER 31

New Start for Women

"Darlene gets a lot of inspiration from her religious beliefs and the spiritual connection she receives guides her through some of these opportunities," said Dr. Al. "She's all about giving people confidence and believes everyone has inside them a golden nugget—and all you have to do is mine it and you can do anything. And she is who she is. I don't see much difference between her public and private personas. She likes to say, 'Living is giving and giving is living,' and it's so true."

Dr. Al is right about my belief in the power of prayer. I usually pray, "God, I'm here to serve you. Show me how you want me to do it.' I had been praying on what I should focus on next and wanted to do more to help underserved women in Ulster County. I am usually in Florida for the winter months and invited Dr. Al, who also has family there, to have lunch with me to discuss some ideas.

Dr. Al reminisced about that conversation: "When Darlene called to say 'There's something I want to talk with you about. Let's have lunch," I flew down to meet with her because when Darlene invites you to lunch, you know something's on her mind. I never turn down a lunch with her," he laughed. "She said, 'I have a need to help women. I know there are single moms who are working two jobs, trying to raise their families and really struggling. What can we do to change this?' I jotted four to six thoughts on my napkin and she said, 'I'm willing to help out here.' I went to my team and that's how we began the New Start for Women program," said Dr. Al.

Kole's office was Dr. Al's next stop. "Dr. Al visited me in my office and sketched out Darlene's idea, asking me and [SUNY

Ulster Associate Vice President for Workforce, Economic Development and Community Partnerships] Chris Marx to flesh it out further and develop next steps," Kole said. "I went to churches, nonprofit organizations, businesses and banks to ask them for input. I did research on the demographics of Ulster County and put together a framework to serve women by helping them to get an education so they would be in a stronger position for economic mobility."

While Mindy Kole and her team were working to develop the project, I continued to discuss my ideas with others. Pat Courtney-Strong, a local entrepreneur and well-connected public advocate who had run for public office and often worked behind the scenes to make things happen in Kingston, called Mindy to say she had heard about the program.

"Pat told me she had mentioned New Start for Women to Peter Buffett, the CEO of the NoVo Foundation," Kole recalled. "Peter had turned it over to his local team and wanted us to come in and do a presentation. I was nervous! Chris Marx and I took our team—SUNY Ulster Vice President for Academic Affairs and Dean of Faculty, Kevin Stoner, and Executive Director of Ulster Community College Foundation, Lorraine Salmon—along with a written presentation we had prepared for them. NoVo gave us a grant to run the program for three years."

"Darlene's $100,000 donation of seed money helped SUNY Ulster secure a $1.5 million grant from the NoVo Foundation," said Dr. Al. "It's a signature program, and the participants have fun, meaningful experiences. The program is changing lives."

In July 2019, New Start for Women (NSW) debuted with 16 enrolled students. Jordan Scruggs, who previously served as assistant pastor at St. James Methodist Church in Kingston, was onboarded to fulfill her new duties as the first director of the program at the same time as the first student cohort orientation. "We were building the plane while we were flying it that first year," she recalled.

Fourteen women completed their Business Certificate in general management with 13 graduating from the program with the aim of attaining a living wage, pursuing their education and achieving economic mobility. The Business Certificate is essentially half of an associate degree and coursework focuses on skills most necessary in a business environment, such as leadership, accounting, communications and networking.

Two NSW graduates received 100 percent full scholarships to continue their education at Bard College, and another received a 75 percent scholarship to attend Marist College. Two graduated with 4.0 GPAs and two enrolled to continue their education in an associate degree program at SUNY Ulster.

In its second year, the program began in the summer of 2020 with 20 students enrolled, but five withdrew due to complications from the COVID-19 pandemic. Currently, 14 are on track to complete their certificate in December of 2021, and a 15th plans to return in the fall after giving birth this spring.

Scruggs met with more than 100 potential candidates for the third year of the program, underlying the precarious nature of the lives of so many Ulster County women. Twenty new students enrolled in the third NSW cohort, which began in the summer of 2021. "Though this is a smaller number than we hoped to enroll, several women deferred admission until 2022 while they get back on their feet following the pandemic," she said. "It's really important to us that the women enrolled are positioned to succeed, and sometimes this means helping them to chart out a trajectory for success that includes delaying enrollment until they are stable enough to concentrate on school.

"We provide temporary resources to alleviate the financial burden that can keep women from getting an education," explained Scruggs. "Many of our participants have tried school before—perhaps while working full-time or raising children—and had to drop out or withdraw. We help them with transportation, childcare costs, electronic access (including borrowed laptops) and with negotiating a lot of bureaucratic systems. I have an advanced degree and it's my full-time job to help people figure this out, and I still find it challenging. Imagine you're a single parent who is trying to negotiate these systems while raising a child and trying not to be homeless. It can be really daunting."

Nonetheless, the program is successful, noted Kole. "We've learned it takes intensive advisement and tremendous support to overcome societal barriers," she said. "We have partnered with Family of Woodstock, a comprehensive non-profit organization that helps our students with their housing and healthcare needs, as well as all the societal issues they face. We run a lot of workshops, do a lot of coaching and handholding, and are fortunate to have the funding to back it all up. All these women need is a break. They're smart, talented, articulate, eager to learn, want better lives for themselves and their children, but they've been crushed by society," Kole added. "They can do wonders—WONDERS—with their lives with this type of support. I want to bring New Start for Women to First Lady Jill Biden. Sustaining and scaling up a vital program like this should not be reliant on getting a grant from a private foundation."

According to Scruggs, the team hopes to build out NSW as a continuing support system. "Women having each other's backs is one of the best ways to turn the tide and break the cycle of poverty," she stated. "Though I received my undergraduate degree at a small college, my graduate degree is from Yale Divinity School, which has really changed my life in that I suddenly have access to this powerful network of people and job references that literally follows me everywhere. I want our program to become that kind of resource for our NSW community," she said.

"We're building our Advisory Board with our graduates, who are deeply invested in the program. I am really impressed by the incredible resiliency, character and commitment of these women," Scruggs continued. "It's particularly moving to see women succeed in this way, especially when they are responsible for raising children, and may have experienced trauma, abuse, addiction and the stressors of poverty too. I have one child and daycare and a supportive partner and I'm still exhausted. The fact that they juggle so much is really amazing. The women in our program are often viewed as statistics, but they are so much more than the 'at-risk' and 'under-resourced' labels our society gives them. I am learning something new from the NSW students every day. They are functioning like champions."

Kole said, "Darlene is a role model in everything I do. Her words and wisdom guide me in my personal and private life, as well as professionally. As the New Start for Women program has developed, I've become so much more deeply mindful of how the problems of society impact the women we serve. My growing awareness of the impact of these problems on learning and education, as well as the reasons why the women are caught in poverty and can't get out, has evolved into an awareness of what's needed. Working with the women in New Start for Women has changed my life. Jordan Scruggs, who is our director, is the perfect person for the job; I play a support role for her and have worked alongside her to get the program on its feet.

"I just admire and love Darlene. She is the most giving person I have ever met in my life, and she has taught me to think more along those lines," Kole admitted. "She's smart—I brag on her all the time and tell my students she was a flight attendant in the 1960s who had to quit her job because she got married. 'This was the 1960s, not the 1860s'—and my female students just look at me. Her position of being a role model for not just my female students but all my students is impressive. She is always one of our OWN It! conference speakers and gives a mini-motivational talk in the morning session. She talks about her life, how blessed she is, how she learned to give, and her grit and persistence.

DARLENE L. PFEIFFER

"With 'fire in the belly,' as Darlene says, you can accomplish anything. She came from not much to become what she is today and is very humble about it. Her involvement with Kentucky Fried Chicken—especially during the years when she led the franchisees to prevail in their lawsuit against PepsiCo—is very inspirational to the women who are part of the New Start for Women program," Kole added. "When she tells stories about her life and the things she was able to do and accomplish, the women in the New Start program and our business students realize they can do more than they think they can. They realize they can achieve more. Darlene and I are both that way, which is why we 'click.' She just says, 'Let's do it' and makes things happen."

However, noted Kole, Darlene's level of giving as a human being is her primary guiding value. "If more people were like that, this could be a perfect world. I relate to her a lot," said Kole, who admits to being a big fan. "I admire her so much—am in awe of her—and she has taught me a lot. I want to be her when I grow up, and I'm not a kid. You keep learning until you're done. We all should be lifelong learners in work, our personal lives, everything. She's very special to me."

Dr. Al cites "consistency" as the attribute that sets me apart from some donors. "In the time I've been here, she's always looking ahead to something new, always looking for the need, trying to solve the problem. And for her, it's not just about giving: It's giving for a purpose. She's a powerful lady, and self-made too. She knows the value of effort and time commitment." He added, with a laugh: "She likes that both of us wake up early, so when the phone rings at 6:00 a.m., I know it's Darlene. Her endurance is amazing, and I hope I can continue to work as tirelessly as she does in making a difference. I admire that."

CHAPTER 32

New Start for Women: Student Profiles

Rachel Collins

When Rachel Collins entered the New Start for Women program in 2019 at age 39, she was 1.5 years into sobriety. In the spring of 2021, she graduated from SUNY Ulster with an associate's degree in applied science with a focus on business and entrepreneurial studies.

Rachel Collins ranked #23 in her class when she graduated from Onteora High School yet considered herself an average student. She tried to go to college twice—enrolling right after high school and again at age 24—but neither experience was good. Collins gave birth to a son at age 22, and in 2008, she finished school in Manhattan and earned her Esthetician license.

"After I got sober, I wanted to return to school. My mother told me about New Start for Women, which was just beginning in 2019," Collins recalled. "The only thing I knew about the program was that it's for women who need a new start and tuition would be paid for completely." After applying, she was placed on a waitlist for 2020, but then an unexpected opening allowed her to start NSW that year during the last week of orientation. "There I was, thrown into school," Collins said. "It was a whirlwind experience."

According to Collins, "I had tried to go to college two times before and failed miserably. I figured 'third time's a charm,' but I had a lot of trepidation. I'd had so much trauma, abuse, struggle and alcoholism in my life, I wondered, 'Can I do this?' It was going to be with a group of women, the bane of my experience as a biracial woman. I'd had several traumatizing experiences with women and didn't know if I was cut out for this."

Yet once she was in the program, Collins overcame her fear of trying new things. She now calls NSW "one of the most amazing experiences in my life, aside from giving birth. I wanted to go to school but didn't know how I would afford it. I wanted to better myself but didn't know how to get it. Based on past experiences, I wondered if I could handle the load. I didn't want to trigger myself into relapsing."

The NSW program allowed Collins to focus on school with no worries about finances. She certainly had some obstacles: She didn't have Internet at her apartment, needed money to buy books, and had expenses for traveling to and from school and her job. "All of it was taken care of," she said. "And not only that, but somebody actually cared about other women and giving back. Darlene Pfeiffer cooked up this idea and I don't know if she knows the depth of what she started. I didn't know I was capable of getting straight As, but it turns out I'm this amazing accountant," said Collins. "Everybody should have a Mindy Kole in their life—she won't give up on you and what you can do for yourself. And Jordan Scruggs? She's in your face with her bright smile and is a life-saving troubleshooter."

The women in Collins' NSW cohort ranged in age from 30 to 65—each one with her own struggles, needs and wants. "We weren't necessarily BFFs, but we respected each other," said Collins. Starting out, she recalled that "one of the women had a hard way about her, and I watched her transform into one of the most giving, loving people. She blossomed into her true self."

Beyond personal growth, the Business Certificate which Collins earned through NSW put her halfway to her associate's degree in applied science. "NSW made it possible for me to finish school. I graduated and walked away with four As and a B+."

But getting good grades wasn't even the best part of the program for Collins. "Even if you don't pass with flying colors, you can look at yourself and say, 'Now I know some accounting'," she said. "Women have to fight against the feminization of poverty if they want to do something for themselves. During my Accounting 101 class, I was always on the phone with my mother, who is an accountant, and that's why I decided to make myself available as an accounting tutor for women in the NSW program."

Now, at age 41, Collins is building upon her profession as an esthetician. She is working on a five-year business plan with Kole's assistance, intends to create a home-based business in her own two-bedroom house and has already purchased her first piece of spa equipment. "I'll look for a job as a manager at a spa to save money and keep myself in the spa industry while I build my business. When I was a waitress, I struggled to save money and spa treatments were too expensive. I want to create a mini-spa that's affordable to your average Joe/Josephine, and I will be successful doing that by the time I'm 45."

NSW offered many emotional as well as professional benefits too. "I enjoy my life—I'm not 100 percent at peace yet but I have never felt this peaceful," said Collins, who described herself as "a work in progress. I work hard to maintain my sobriety and I have a good therapist. Who would have thought there are so many emotions when you can't hide behind alcohol? I try to tell everybody about this program. It is a lifesaver. I'm finally doing something for myself and it's an empowering feeling."

In just a few semesters, Collins said, "I learned more than I ever knew. I learned how to properly write a business email. I know more about marketing and can draw up a business plan and Excel spreadsheets. I have management skills, human resources skills. I tell women to take advantage of the resources provided. I kept feeling it was too good to be true, waiting for the other shoe to drop, thinking something's going to hit me; I'll have to pay. But I had nothing to worry about. Even if earning a degree doesn't fit into your career path, it can't hurt to have some managerial skills. You can apply a general Certificate in Business to the position you're in now and rise to the top. You just have to show up. It's a powerful program, a blessing and a lifesaver."

Samantha Wolven
Samantha Wolven, 33, will graduate from SUNY Ulster with her Business Certificate from the New Start for Women program in December 2021. She grew up in Woodstock and has lived in Kingston for the past 12 years.

"I never knew what I wanted to be when I was younger, and I was not going on the right path," said Samantha Wolven. "I was an addict for a long time, and the New Start for Women program helped me find myself and who I am. It's a process to find out where your heart lies and what you want to do, and I'm pretty sure I've come to the conclusion I enjoy helping people."

As Wolven finished her third semester at the end of 2021, she planned to continue her work at SUNY Ulster to earn an associate's degree and then transfer to SUNY New Paltz to pursue a bachelor's degree in human services. "I'd like to work with teens who are not in the best situation and show them, by being a good role model, they can do it too," she explained. "I have a story I can share, and sometimes people ask me, 'How did you do that and how can you be so open about the past?' When somebody who is like I was hears my story, they may realize they don't have to be scared and they can overcome too. That's my goal right now."

"My childhood was pretty rough," Wolven continued. "I was raised by a single mom who had her own addictions. In school, I was kind of a bad student, got in with the wrong crowd, and started dropping out. I had no self-worth. I didn't think education was for me. I didn't fit in, had emotional disorders and found it difficult to be in class."

Once she got clean, Wolven got a job working at a hotel. "I was miserable but I thought I had to accept it—'You made your bed' kind of thing'," she said. "I was a human being but not the happiest person in the world. If it wasn't for New Start for Women, I would never have imagined my life as it is now. The program brought something out in me. I needed the support from the other ladies and from Jordan, and now I know I can hold on until I'm ready to go out on my own. It's amazing."

Wolven met Darlene Pfeiffer over Zoom. "She's a wonderful person. She came to our classes twice—once so we could meet her and tell her about ourselves, and another time she just observed our class."

After two semesters, Wolven had finished classes in principles of management and accounting along with a computer class focused on business communications and business computer (including Word, Excel and PowerPoint). "I made it through accounting and am proud of myself—I learned quite a bit," she added. Her third and final semester will be focused on leadership and an internship of her choosing. "I will graduate in December and it's super exciting!"

"With Zoom classes, it was a little tricky," she admitted. "We were all very patient with each other and made it work. Because of the pandemic, I was going a little crazy from not interacting with people. It was pretty rough, and I was scared to leave the house, but I needed people interaction and it worked out."

Her experience at SUNY Ulster has made her "feel like a newborn child," Wolven said. "I needed somebody to hold my hand, and am grateful for NSW, even though I can't see where life is going to take me. I owe NSW so much and feel so blessed. I never believed in myself before, but people—here at NSW and in the drug/alcohol program—believed in me before I knew how to believe in myself. This is a great opportunity for any woman, because it teaches you how to move forward, be independent and it gives you support before you jump into anything. I hadn't been in school for years and couldn't have done this without the support from NSW."

Jill Pacheco
Jill Pacheco, 39, is currently enrolled in the New Start for Women (NSW) program with one semester to go. She will earn her Business Certificate by the end of 2021. Born and raised in Kingston, she and her husband have three teenage children.

Jill Pacheco wasn't ready for college at age 18 when she tried it for one semester immediately after graduating from Kingston High School. She became pregnant at age 20 and spent many years as a stay-at-home mom as well as volunteering, and then became a teacher's assistant, at a daycare center—an experience she described as "kind of a burnout job." As she tells it, "I felt torn. I was helping all these other kids, but my daughter was having a hard time reading at school, so I stopped working. I had to do a lot to get her the help she needs."

Pacheco got a new job in a doctor's office, but it ended when the pandemic hit. "I kept thinking to myself, 'If she closes the office, I've got no experience or skills to take anywhere. I don't have a degree or anything,'" she recalled. Then her son came across New Start for Women's Facebook page and told her about it. Pacheo connected with the director of NSW, Jordan Scruggs, and was accepted into the program.

"I was very nervous," she admitted. "I had been out of school for 20 years and was always the type of student who just got by. Even if I didn't understand something, I was pushed through. But the NSW program offers the support you need so you are successful. I needed to take this leap.

"Now that my kids are older, I work so much harder because they are watching me," she said. "My son is seventeen and I have a lot of expectations for him. I tell him, 'You're going to go to college,' but how can I have those expectations for him if I don't do it for myself? Seeing me do this is helping

DREAM BIG, ADD MOXIE

my children."

Pacheco even finished her most challenging semester with flying colors. "I always had bad math anxiety when I was in school before, but I did it!" she said. "I got an A! Having the support from the program really pushed me through."

One of her biggest challenges—"besides math," she says—was gaining familiarity with the computer. "There were so many things I learned that I didn't know. During the pandemic, navigating Zoom was a little challenging but certainly do-able," she said. But an even bigger hurdle was learning to put herself first. Before NSW, Pacheco said she always had the feeling her kids should be her main focus. But that's no longer the case.

"My job now is to see them through. Taking time away from them to do my studying is going to benefit them, all of us. They're watching," she said. "My advice to other women is to give yourself a chance. The program is going to work but you have to make yourself available to it. And I'd say, it's never too late. Take this leap. There were fourteen women in my cohort, including myself, and you do bond. We help each other so we all get through."

Although Pacheco said she's never met Darlene Pfeiffer in person, she did "meet her over Zoom. She popped into one of our classes. I just feel incredibly thankful for this opportunity. It's about so much more than earning grades. I feel like I'm becoming a different person."

In August 2021, Pacheco began a part-time job as a student aide in the NSW office, where she was able to use the things she had learned so far—"about time management, for example, and I helped put the paperwork together for the new cohort coming in."

For her next step, after earning a Certificate in General Business Management, Pacheco's torn between earning an associate's degree and getting her foot in the door with a nonprofit job. "People have helped me, and I would like to give back," she said. "I want to help people get the help they need."

CHAPTER 33

Going Forward

"Darlene Pfeiffer is nothing short of a trailblazer," said Lorraine Salmon, executive director, Ulster Community College Foundation. "This magnanimous entrepreneur has built a philanthropic and entrepreneurial legacy fueled by her passion for women and education.

"Darlene is strategically involved in numerous charitable organizations throughout the region, regularly giving to community food programs such as the Clinton Avenue United Methodist Church's Annual Thanksgiving Day dinner, and is a donor and board director of the Community Foundations of the Hudson Valley.

"In 2010," she continued, "Darlene joined the Ulster Community College Foundation, Inc.'s Board of Directors and in 2012, the Darlene L. Pfeiffer Center for Entrepreneurial Studies opened at SUNY Ulster. At the time, her donation for the center was the single-largest gift and pledge to the community college by a living donor, earning her recognition from the New York Community College Trustees with the Benefactor Vision for Tomorrow Award.

"In 2015, the SUNY Ulster OWN It! Entrepreneurial Women's Conference was launched. The annual event, sponsored through Darlene's contributions and vision, has galvanized and energized the community of women entrepreneurs serving some 500 women to date.

"Darlene was also the originating contributor for SUNY Ulster's Pfeiffer Technology and Innovation Lab, which opened in September 2017. The Pfeiffer Lab is a member of the SMARTT (SUNY Manufacturing Alliance for Research and

Technology Transfer) Lab network.

"In 2018, Darlene was only the second recipient to receive the foundation's Your Promise Their Future Award which acknowledges donors who, 'by substantial planned gifts, or generous contributions provide future or present-day funding deemed to be transformative.' At the time, Darlene was providing $15,000 in annual scholarships to students of SUNY Ulster, many of whom were single parents, and had been supporting Ulster students for some 15 years.

"Darlene's scholarship giving has topped $110,000 and has assisted nearly 100 students with persisting with their education. Darlene has used her influence and passion for the community to support a remarkable amount of entrepreneurship and innovation at SUNY Ulster and in our broader Ulster County Community," Salmon added.

Scholarships Given:
- The Darlene L. Pfeiffer Scholarship
- The SUNY Ulster Second Year Scholarship by Darlene L. Pfeiffer
- Daniel Perez Cueva Scholarship for Immigrants by Darlene L. Pfeiffer
- SUNY Ulster Foundation Scholarships in Memory of Andrew Dalstream, Vincent P. DeLuca, Ellen Dubin, Valerie Adamcyk Colby and Anita Peck.

"Darlene is SUNY Ulster's top donor and her impact on our community college is immeasurable," Salmon stated.

"In the 17 years that Darlene has dedicated herself to the community and students of SUNY Ulster, she has contributed more than $1,800,000 in vital scholarships and program funding, including the President's Challenge Scholarship. She has given the Foundation a $1,000,000 planned gift and has made gifts of more than six-figures in total to the Foundation's Gala and unrestricted funds as well as to launch the Darlene L. Pfeiffer Center for Entrepreneurial Studies; the Pfeiffer Technology & Innovation Lab (leading to investments

DARLENE L. PFEIFFER

in SUNY Ulster totaling some $9,500,000); and the New Start for Women Program Powered by Darlene Pfeiffer (leading to $1,500,000 in support from the NoVo Foundation)."

SUNY Ulster students, graduates, alumni, faculty and staff featured in SUNY Ulster's Darlene L. Pfeiffer Center for Entrepreneurial Studies 2018 video.

· 194 ·

CHAPTER 34

The President's Challenge Scholarship

The lives of the students who participate will be changed forever.
— Dr. Alan P. Roberts, President, SUNY Ulster

On June 24, 2021, I presented a $1,000,000 check as an endowment to support the President's Challenge Scholarship (PCS) at SUNY Ulster. This innovative program was designed by Dr. Alan P. Roberts (aka Dr. Al) to assist first-generation college-bound high school students living in Ulster County by helping them to overcome the financial barriers associated with attending college. Students are identified in the eighth grade by sponsoring school districts to receive guidance counseling and mentoring through the completion of high school and are awarded a two-year tuition-free college education at SUNY Ulster.

The President's Challenge Scholarship was launched in 2016 with six eighth-grade students from Rondout Valley Central School District. Today, thanks to a generous community of donors, nearly 200 students are enrolled in the program, and an additional 50 college-bound students join each year from all nine Ulster County school districts.

"There is no way to describe the ongoing impact Darlene's gift has on the potential 50 students annually who will earn this scholarship," said Lorraine Salmon, executive director of the Ulster Community College Foundation. "Darlene is a life changer."

DARLENE L. PFEIFFER

*The people you give to now will outlive you,
and however you give will influence their lives.*

I believe when we give, we live more fully.

When we give, we live completely.

When we give, we live more joyously.

And when we give, we live eternally.

— Darlene L. Pfeiffer

I pray every day and read the Positive Daily Word *and* Positive Christianity *daily entries on the website, Unityonlineradio.org. Living positively is often as simple as shifting your perspective. Each day, usually before I arise from my bed, I start my day with the right attitude—the attitude of gratitude.*

— Darlene L. Pfeiffer

SERVE
I share my gifts in service to others.

The love of God that lives in my heart inspires me to be of service. Today I open my mind to new ideas and the belief that I can make a positive difference.

Service can manifest in small ways and have a large effect. Acts of service carry with them a consciousness of oneness with others, with nature, with God. If I question my ability to make a difference, I remember what it feels like when someone helps me. A connection occurs, a lifting of spirit, a feeling of warmth.

I look for new ways to serve. It could be through prayer, smiles, errands, monetary contributions, the sharing of food, deep listening—the list goes on. Service is love in action and a wonderful way to share my divine gifts.

Like good stewards of the manifold grace of God, serve one another with whatever gift each of you has received.
— 1 Peter 4:10

unityonlineradio.org
Daily Word
Friday, May 28, 2021

APPENDIX

A Lifetime of Living Fearlessly

PART ONE: THE EARLY YEARS

- **1937** October 6 – Darlene Large is born in Columbus, Ohio.
- **1945** Darlene decides she wants to become a flight attendant.
- **1950** Colonel Sanders starts his KFC franchises.

    Darlene's father, Otto Large, dies.

    In high school – enrolls in Andre Correlli Modeling School, Columbus.
- **1952** Darlene gets her first job as a checkout girl at Kroger's.
- **1953** Darlene begins her second job at Beneficial Finance and works there about two years.
- **1955** Darlene graduates West High School as Valedictorian.
- **1956** Darlene enrolls at Capital University in Columbus and receives the Philip Bruck Fleming Scholarship for two years.

PART TWO: THE TWA YEARS

- **1957** Darlene applies to become a flight attendant. She is accepted in August and begins a 30-day training program in December 1957 in Kansas City.
- **1958** Darlene moves to NYC, gets an apartment in Queens and starts flying at age 20.
- **1959** Becomes Supervisor of Flight Attendants (the youngest-ever).
- **1950s, 60s and 70s** Early development of the fast food industry and interstate highway system in the U.S.
- **1960** Bevy Stoll is born.

    Darlene meets Jake Gottlieb.
- **1961** January – Darlene's ruptured appendix results in her missing the John F. Kennedy Inauguration with Jake, who had received an invitation to all the festivities.
- **1962** Colonel Sanders patents his method of pressure frying chicken.
- **1963** Colonel Sanders trademarks the phrase "finger lickin good".

A LIFETIME OF LIVING FEARLESSLY

1964 Darlene is subpoenaed to appear at Federal Grand Jury and testify about her relationship with Jake.

October 25 – Attends the Ed Sullivan Show with her mother (debut of The Rolling Stones in America).

There are now more than 600 KFC locations internationally.

1965 November 9 – While flying on a TWA plane returning to NYC, the East Coast Blackout occurs, a harrowing experience.

November 23 – Darlene weds Jan Headlee and couldn't fly anymore since TWA's policies required flight attendants to be unmarried.

PART THREE: THE KFC YEARS

1965 KFC franchisees in the Southeastern United States establish the first regional group of franchisees.

1967 Darlene purchases her KFC franchises—but has to sign over 51% of ownership to her husband due to archaic bank practices re: women owning businesses and receiving bank loans.

Darlene hires 15-year-old Peter Stoll as one of her first KFC employees.

April – Darlene meets Paul DeLisio when she opens first KFC store in Kingston. Paul is a new insurance agent, and sells her a health insurance/employee benefits package.

1968 Darlene tells Nancy Stoll (who had terminal cancer) she will care for her 8-year-old daughter, Bevy Stoll, after her death.

1970 Bevy and Peter Stoll come to live with Darlene and, when Peter begins to attend Ulster Community College, she helps him get a nearby apartment.

1972 G&K Settlement allows KFC franchisees to purchase supplies in the open market, which reduces the corporate KFC profit margin.

Jake Gottlieb dies.

1973 KFC franchisees in the Northeast region establish a regional group under the leadership of Don Hines.

1974 The Association of KFC Franchisees (AKFCF) forms to unite KFC franchisees and to protect and advance their interests.

1975 Darlene separates from her husband, Jan.

Bevy starts school at Emma Willard in Troy, NY.

APPENDIX

1976 Darlene graduates summa cum laude from SUNY New Paltz with a degree in political science.

KFC Franchise Agreement aka "The 5 Ps" (royalty rate, protected area, ad fee rate, successive renewal and transferability) is created.

The initial meeting of the Northeast KFC franchisee group is held in Bermuda, and Don Hines is elected president.

1977 January – Darlene gets divorced from Jan. She gains control of three of their nine stores in the settlement, as well as $140,000 in debt stemming from Jan's poor management of her businesses.

Bevy graduates from high school, and while working at KFC, begins dating Walt. She leaves KFC, marries Walt in December and the couple moves to Florida.

Darlene attends her first Northeast regional AKFCF meeting. When Don Hines steps down, Darlene is elected to fill all four officer positions.

Darlene calls Shirley Topmiller, Colonel Sanders' secretary, to book his first visit to her Kingston KFC store.

December 24 – Darlene marries Wallace "Wally" Pfeiffer.

1978 Colonel Sanders comes to Darlene's Kingston KFC.

May – Darlene convenes the first regional Northeast AKFCF meeting in Connecticut. To raise funds to pay the franchisees' association fees, she charges vendors an exhibitor fee of $500 for card table space. This gathering establishes the value of networking and collaborating among franchisees and vendors.

1979 The AKFCF Southeast region suggests the AKFCF form the KFC National Purchasing Cooperative to assure low-cost purchase of equipment and supplies (following on success of G&K Settlement).

Early 1980s Regular regional AKFCF meetings increase networking, bonding and communication among franchisees.

1980 Colonel Sanders comes to Darlene's Poughkeepsie KFC.

The AKFCF establishes an eight-page newsletter to disseminate regional meeting minutes and other information relevant to KFC franchisees.

1980 – 1983 Following the Flight Attendants' Union settlement of their sex discrimination lawsuit against the airline industry, Darlene returns to flying at TWA on full-time basis so she can obtain her full pension while running her KFC businesses.

A LIFETIME OF LIVING FEARLESSLY

- **1983** AKFCF establishes the first comprehensive, region-by-region franchisee mailing list.

  Darlene's mother dies.

- **1984** A Memorandum of Agreement is established to specify no changes could be made to the franchisee contracts outlined in the 1976 Franchise Agreement without prior review by legal counsel and the National Franchisee Advisory Council (NFAC).

- **1986** PepsiCo purchases KFC from RJ Reynolds for $840 million. By now, franchisees are accustomed to corporate takeovers and this at first appeared to be just one more in a succession of them. AKFCF hires a new lawyer, Andy Selden.

- **1988** Darlene becomes the first woman to serve as president of the AKFCF (and had automatic seat on the NAC too). Andy Selden has been working with the franchisees for six months at this time.

- **1989** The franchisees enter into 7-year lawsuit in Federal Court against PepsiCo. PepsiCo wanted to change provisions in the 1976 Franchise Agreement and 1984 Memorandum of Agreement, and the majority of the franchisees signed onto the lawsuit.

- **Late 1980s** Darlene establishes the *AKFCF Quarterly* with Webb Howell. The four-color, glossy magazine includes full page ads from vendors, and Darlene uses it to communicate with franchisees about the lawsuit.

- **1991** PepsiCo refuses at last minute to sponsor the annual franchisees' convention in Las Vegas because the lawsuit had become acrimonious. Darlene relocates the convention to Florida and invites Margaret Sanders, the Colonel's daughter, to be keynote speaker. The convention is a success and raises considerable funds for the lawsuit.

- **1995** Darlene becomes the first person to serve two terms as president of the AKFCF when elected to her second term.

- **1997** The AKFCF's lawsuit with PepsiCo is settled. The franchisees retain their right of territorial control. The settlement also merges the NAC and NFAC into one newly formed National Council and Advertising Coop (NCAC), an entity composed of 13 franchisees and 5 corporate members, which protects the decisionmaking advantages of franchisees.

- **2000** Darlene owns three KFCs in Kingston and Poughkeepsie and also serves as VP of the KFC National Advertising Co-op (NAC). She wants to expand the KFC Colonel Sanders Scholarship program.

APPENDIX

- **2002** January 21 – Wally Pfeiffer dies; he and Darlene were married 25 years.

  Darlene becomes more involved with Paul DeLisio.

- **2004** Darlene raises $1 million at the KFC Convention to expand the KFC Colonel Sanders Scholarship Program.

  ### PART FOUR: THE SUNY ULSTER YEARS

- **2005** Darlene initiates discussions with SUNY Ulster President Don Katt and SUNY Ulster Foundation Director Marianne Collins about helping students in need.

  Darlene beings to support SUNY Ulster's scholarship programs by establishing five in her name at $1,000/per student. By 2021, she is giving ten of these scholarships annually.

- **2007** Sean Alvarez becomes the first Ulster County student to receive the KFC Colonel Sanders Scholarship.

- **2010** Darlene is invited to join the SUNY Ulster Foundation board of directors.

- **Around 2010** Darlene offers $100,000 to SUNY Ulster to establish an Entrepreneurial Center on campus. Funds are used to renovate the Center and underwrite additional costs to bring part-time adjunct professor Mindy Kole on-board full-time for three years to ensure the success of the growing Business Studies Department.

- **2011** Darlene initiates the "Start Here Go Far Boutique" on SUNY Ulster campus. It provides gently used quality clothing for students who don't have proper attire to attend professional functions or job interviews.

  The grand opening ceremonies and ribbon cutting are held for the Darlene L. Pfeiffer Center for Entrepreneurial Studies and SUNY Chancellor Nancy Zimpher attends.

- **2012** Spring – The SUNY Ulster Entrepreneurial Studies Certificate program begins in tandem with the opening of the Center.

- **2013** Peter Stoll dies of a heart attack at age 60.

- **2015** Dr. Alan P. Roberts (aka "Dr. Al") becomes President of SUNY Ulster.

  SUNY Ulster's OWN it! Entrepreneurial Women's Conference launches with Darlene as an important supporter.

A LIFETIME OF LIVING FEARLESSLY

2017 Gala celebrating Darlene's 50th year as a KFC franchisee.

Grand opening of the Pfeiffer Technology & Innovation Lab at SUNY Ulster. Darlene donated $100,000 in seed money to retrofit existing building, acquire 3-D printers and computers and underwrite additional costs.

2018 Darlene is named recipient of the Ulster Community College Foundation's "Your Promise Their Future Award," which recognizes donors who "by substantial planned gifts, or generous contributions provide future or present-day funding deemed to be transformative."

2019 Darlene sells her KFC stores and retires from KFC.

Darlene provides seed money ($100,000) to begin New Start for Women at SUNY Ulster. Her support helps attract $1.5 million from The NoVo Foundation to develop the program over the next three years.

2021 Darlene contributes $1,000,000 to an endowment fund to support the President's Challenge Scholarship.

Darlene advocates to increase statewide earnings for home health care workers and continues to support training programs for home health care workers through New Start for Women.

Front row – Walt & Bevy Hung, Darlene, Joey Longo.
Back row – Paul DeLisio, Nick Pfeiffer. On a cruise circa 2010.

APPENDIX

Credits

WRITING AND EDITING
Debra Bresnan

COVER DESIGN
Rachel Ake Kuech

BOOK DESIGN AND PRODUCTION
Rick Whelan, Ditto! Design!

PHOTOS
Pg. vii   Photographer: Michael Gold
Pg. 19   TWA Flight Center by littleny
Pg. 60   Darlene speaking at AKFCF convention provided by Central Iowa KFC Inc
Pgs. 120, 126 Provided by Central Iowa KFC Inc
Pg. 147   Provided by Anreka Gordon
Pg. 150   Unknown
Pg. 157   Provided by Christine Fautz
Pg. 158   Photographers clockwise from top: Ilene Cutler, Kerri Vitek, Ilene Cutler, Ilene Cutler
Pg. 159   Photographers top: Kerri Vitek; bottom: Lorraine Salmon
Pg. 160   Photographers top: Kerri Vitek; bottom: John Halpern
Pg. 175   Photographer: Kerri Vitek
Pg. 178   Photographer: Kerri Vitek
Pg. 194   Photographers: John Halpern and Ilene Cutler

All other photos provided by Darlene L. Pfeiffer